Classic Australian Poems

Edited by
Christopher Cheng

Illustrated by
Gregory Rogers

RANDOM HOUSE AUSTRALIA

Contents

Introduction			4
1.	Andy's Gone with Cattle	Henry Lawson	8
2.	The Ant Explorer	CJ Dennis	10
3.	The Australian Slanguage	WT Goodge	12
4.	A Ballad of Shearing (Shearing at Castlereagh)	Banjo Paterson	14
5.	Bell-birds	Henry Kendall	16
6.	Brumby's Run	Banjo Paterson	18
7.	A Bush Christening	Banjo Paterson	20
8.	A Bush Christmas	CJ Dennis	22
9.	The Circus	CJ Dennis	25
10.	Clancy of the Overflow	Banjo Paterson	26
11.	The Days of Cobb & Co.	GM Smith (Steele Grey)	28
12.	The Digger's Song	Barcroft Henry Boake	30
13.	An Exile's Farewell	Adam Lindsay Gordon	32
14.	Freedom on the Wallaby	Henry Lawson	34
15.	Fur and Feathers	Banjo Paterson	36
16.	The Geebung Polo Club	Banjo Paterson	38
17.	Going to School	CJ Dennis	41
18.	Hist!	CJ Dennis	42
19.	How M'Dougal Topped the Score	Thomas E Spencer	44
20.	The Last of His Tribe	Henry Kendall	48
21.	The Lights of Cobb and Co.	Henry Lawson	50
22.	The Man from Ironbark	Banjo Paterson	54
23.	The Man from Snowy River	Banjo Paterson	56
24.	Mr Smith	DH Souter	62
25.	Mulga Bill's Bicycle	Banjo Paterson	64
26.	My Typewriter	Edward Dyson	66
27.	Native Companions Dancing	John Shaw Neilson	67
28.	Old Granny Sullivan	John Shaw Neilson	68
29.	Old Man Platypus	Banjo Paterson	72
30.	On the Night Train	Henry Lawson	73

#	Title	Author	Page
31.	'Ough!'	WT Goodge	74
32.	The Pieman	CJ Dennis	75
33.	Pioneers	Frank Hudson	76
34.	Pioneers	Banjo Paterson	77
35.	Pitchin' at the Church	PJ Hartigan (John O'Brien)	78
36.	Poets	CJ Dennis	80
37.	Post-Hole Mick	GM Smith (Steele Grey)	82
38.	The Roaring Days	Henry Lawson	84
39.	A Ruined Reversolet	CJ Dennis	88
40.	Said Hanrahan	PJ Hartigan (John O'Brien)	90
41.	Santa Claus in the Bush	Banjo Paterson	94
42.	The Shearer's Wife	Louis Esson	98
43.	A Snake Yarn	WT Goodge	100
44.	Song of the Artesian Waters	Banjo Paterson	101
45.	The Swagman	CJ Dennis	104
46.	Tangmalangaloo	PJ Hartigan (John O'Brien)	106
47.	The Teacher	CJ Dennis	108
48.	The Teams	Henry Lawson	110
49.	The Tram-Man	CJ Dennis	112
50.	The Traveller	CJ Dennis	114
51.	The Travelling Post-Office	Banjo Paterson	116
52.	The Triantiwontigongolope	CJ Dennis	118
53.	Waiting for the Rain (A Shearing Song)	John Neilson	120
54.	Waltzing Matilda	Banjo Paterson	122
55.	Waratah and Wattle	Henry Lawson	124
56.	The Warrigal	Henry Kendall	126
57.	Where the Dead Men Lie	Barcroft Henry Boake	128
58.	Where the Pelican Builds	Mary Hannay Foott	132
59.	The Women of the West	George Essex Evans	134
60.	Woolloomooloo	CJ Dennis	136

Poet Biographies		137
Book References		148
Index of First Lines		150
Index of Poets		152

Introduction

I love stories, both writing them and reading them. I was privileged enough to attend a primary school where we were encouraged to play with words and where poetry was very much a part of our classroom. Sometimes we would begin lessons with words from some of the great Australian poets. Many of these belonged to our teachers' personal collections of poems—the ones that they really loved. We too were encouraged to collect the poems that we really loved.

Our teachers would write the poems onto the chalkboard and we would copy the words into our poetry books (combining handwriting lessons with English lessons). Sometimes the teachers would print the poems that they had themselves carefully copied for us. We would glue the pages into our poetry books and decorate them with our own illustrations (which was often a homework task too). I kept the poems but ditched my attempts at illustrations . . . Gregory Rogers's illustrations are much better! Often we would learn the poems (that was another homework task) and at the end of the week our class would recite the week's new verse, another that we had memorised to perfection. Many school assemblies featured a class reciting poetry. Sometimes we even entered competitions reciting this wonderful Australian poetry.

The ballads and poems in this book are just like very short stories written in rhyming verse. When the poets were creating these poems they were often writing to explain the life that they saw around them or that they remembered . . . a very different Australia from the one we now live in.

The poets were creating word-pictures of the environment and the landscape and the people they saw.

At the turn of the last century some of our most popular poets were employed by the major newspapers to travel around the country and report on 'life on the land'. Other poets simply travelled from town to town under their own steam and wrote of the life, as they saw it, in ballads and verse. Many of the poems in this collection are from those times.

- Some of the poems are funny—just try to read 'Mulga Bill's Bicycle' without giggling at the crazy antics of an over-confident person trying to learn to ride a pushbike and who ends up in the creek.

- Some of them are serious—read 'The Women of the West' or 'Pioneers' to see how much of a struggle that life was.

- Other poets such as PJ Hartigan (John O'Brien) are able to treat a serious subject like drought with humour and fun, as he does in 'Said Hanrahan'.

- And some of the poems are wonderful ways of playing with words.
  So Tri-
      Tri-anti-wonti-
          Triantiwontigongolope.

In this book there are poems about the land, about the animals of the bush, about life in the city and the country (and sometimes about the vast differences between them), about 'mateship' and friendship, about personalities, and I have also included some simply silly, funny poems.

Over the years some of these poems, such as 'The Man from Snowy River' and 'Hist!', have been so popular that picture book illustrators have won awards for creating artwork to accompany the verse, in books of their own.

Some of the poems in this book have extra verses, or slightly different words from those we are used to. This is because many of the poems that I have chosen are in their original (or near-to-original) form, the way they were first published in the newspapers or journals. Many of these poems were written for specific publications. In many cases the poems were subsequently collated (sometimes after the poet's death) and slightly altered by editors or publishers.

Why do I like these poems and ballads? I enjoy the rhyme and the rhythm. I also like them because I can read these words and then jump into my mind and imagine what the characters were doing and I can imagine what the poet was writing about. And I enjoy the way that each poem or ballad tells a complete story of a time in Australia's recent history when the life that people lived was so very much different from the more comfortable and chaotic life that we live now—and it is a life that we must remember.

Poetry is fun. It is a wonderful way of expressing thoughts and feelings and impressions in mostly short grabs, so . . .

Read the poems and laugh.

Read the poems and be moved.

Read the poems to recite.

Read the poems to enjoy.

Read the poems, and then why not write your own!

CHRISTOPHER CHENG
www.chrischeng.com

Andy's Gone with Cattle

Henry Lawson

Our Andy's gone to battle now
'Gainst Drought, the red marauder;
Our Andy's gone with cattle now
Across the Queensland border.

He's left us in dejection now;
Our hearts with him are roving.
It's dull on this selection now—
Since Andy went a-droving.

Who now shall wear the cheerful face
In times when things are slackest?
And who shall whistle round the place
When Fortune frowns her blackest?

Oh, who shall 'cheek' the squatter now
When he comes round us snarling?
His tongue is growing hotter now
Since Andy cross'd the Darling.

The gates are out of order now
Each wind the riders rattle;
For far far across the border now
Our Andy's gone with cattle.

Poor Aunty's looking thin and white;
And Uncle's cross with worry;
And poor old 'Blucher' howls all night
Since Andy left Macquarie.

ANDY'S GONE WITH CATTLE

Oh, may the showers in torrents fall,
And all the tanks run over;
And may the grass grow green and tall
In pathways of the drover!

And may good angels send the rain
On desert stretches sandy;
And when the summer comes again
God grant 'twill bring us Andy!

Australian Town and Country Journal, 1888

> In 1966, when Australia first issued decimal currency, an image of Henry Lawson, along with scenes from his childhood in Gulgong, decorated the back of the Australian $10 paper note.

The Ant Explorer

CJ Dennis

Once a little sugar ant made up his mind to roam—
To fare away far away, far away from home.
He had eaten all his breakfast, and he had his Ma's consent
To see what he should chance to see; and here's the way he went—
Up and down a fern frond, round and round a stone,
Down a gloomy gully where he loathed to be alone,
Up a mighty mountain range, seven inches high,
Through the fearful forest grass that nearly hid the sky,
Out along a bracken bridge, bending in the moss,
Till he reached a dreadful desert that was feet and feet across.
'Twas a dry, deserted desert, and a trackless land to tread;
He wished that he was home again and tucked-up tight in bed.
His little legs were wobbly, his strength was nearly spent,
And so he turned around again; and here's the way he went—
Back away from desert lands, feet and feet across,
Back along the bracken bridge bending in the moss,
Through the fearful forest grass, shutting out the sky,
Up a mighty mountain range seven inches high,
Down a gloomy gully, where he loathed to be alone,
Up and down a fern frond and round and round a stone.
A dreary ant, a weary ant, resolved no more to roam,
He staggered up the garden path and popped back home.

A Book for Kids, 1921

THE ANT EXPLORER

The Australian Slanguage

WT Goodge

'Tis the everyday Australian
Has a language of his own,
Has a language, or a slanguage,
Which can simply stand alone;
And a 'dickon pitch to kid us'
Is a synonym for 'lie,'
And to 'nark it' means to stop it,
And to 'nit it' means to fly.

And a bosom friend's a 'cobber,'
And a horse a 'prad' or 'moke,'
While a casual acquaintance
Is a 'joker' or a 'bloke.'
And his lady-love's his 'donah'
Or his 'clinah' or his 'tart'
Or his 'little bit o' muslin,'
As it used to be his 'bart.'

And his naming of the coinage
Is a mystery to some,
With his 'quid' and 'half-a-caser'
And his 'deener' and his 'scrum!'
And a 'tin-back' is a party
Who's remarkable for luck,
And his food is called his 'tucker'
Or his 'panem' or his 'chuck.'

A policeman is a 'johnny'
Or a 'copman' or a 'trap,'
And a thing obtained on credit
Is invariably 'strap.'

A conviction's known as 'trouble,'
And a gaol is called a 'jug,'
And a sharper is a 'spieler,'
And a simpleton's a 'tug.'

If he hits a man in fighting
That is what he calls a 'plug,'
If he borrows money from you
He will say he 'bit your lug.'
And to 'shake it' is to steal it,
And to 'strike it' is to beg,
And a jest is 'poking borac'
And a jester 'pulls your leg.'

Things are 'cronk' when they go wrongly
In the language of the 'push,'
But when things go as he wants 'em
He declares it is 'all cush.'
When he's bright he's got a 'napper,'
And he's 'ratty' when he's daft,
And when looking for employment
He is 'out o' blooming graft.'

And his clothes he calls his 'clobber'
Or his 'togs', but what of that
When a 'castor' or a 'kady'
Is the name he gives his hat!
And our undiluted English
Is a fad to which we cling,
But the great Australian slanguage
Is a truly awful thing!

The Bulletin, 1898

A Ballad of Shearing*

Banjo Paterson

The bell is set a-ringing and the engine gives a toot,
There's five-and-thirty shearers here are shearing for the loot,
So stir yourselves, you penners-up, and shove the sheep along,
The musterers are fetching them a hundred-thousand strong;
And make your collie dogs speak up—what *would*
   the buyers say
In London if the wool was late this year from Castlereagh!

The man that rang the Tubbo shed is not the ringer here,
That stripling from the Cooma side can teach him how
   to shear;
They trim away the ragged locks—and *rip* the cutter goes
And leaves a track of snowy wool from brisket to the nose.
It's lovely how they peel it off with never stop nor stay—
They're racing for the ringer's place this year at Castlereagh.

The man that keeps the cutters sharp is growling in his cage,
He's always in a hurry and he's always in a rage.
'You clumsy-fisted mutton-heads, you'd make a fellow sick,
You pass yourselves as shearers—you were born to swing a pick;
Another broken cutter here, that's two you've broke to-day—
It's awful how such crawlers come to shear at Castlereagh.'

The youngsters picking up the fleece enjoy the merry din
They throw the classer up the fleece, he throws it to the bin.
The pressers standing in their box are waiting for the wool,
There's room for just a couple more, the press is nearly full.
Now jump upon the lever, lads, and heave and heave away,
Another bale of snowy fleece is branded 'Castlereagh.'

From South and East the shearers come across the Overland,
Upon the slopes of Southern hills their little homesteads stand,
And all day long with desperate haste they're shearing for their lives,
The cheque they earn at Castlereagh brings comfort to their wives.
So may each shearer tally up a hundred sheep a day,
And every year obtain a shed as good as Castlereagh.

The Bulletin, 1894

* *In some books and other publications this is known as 'Shearing at Castlereagh'. The last stanza is often not included in collections.*

Bell-birds

Henry Kendall

By channels of coolness the echoes are calling,
And down the dim gorges I hear the creek falling;
It lives in the mountain, where moss and the sedges
Touch with their beauty the banks and the ledges;
Through brakes of the cedar and sycamore bowers
Struggles the light that is love to the flowers.
And, softer than slumber, and sweeter than singing,
The notes of the bell-birds are running and ringing.

The silver-voiced bell-birds, the darlings of day-time,
They sing in September their songs of the May-time.
When shadows wax strong, and the thunder-bolts hurtle,
They hide with their fear in the leaves of the myrtle;
When rain and the sunbeams shine mingled together
They start up like fairies that follow fair weather,
And straightway the hues of their feathers unfolden
Are the green and the purple, the blue and the golden.

BELL-BIRDS

October, the maiden of bright
  yellow tresses,
Loiters for love in these cool
  wildernesses;
Loiters knee-deep in the grasses,
  to listen,
Where dripping rocks gleam and
  the leafy pools glisten.
Then is the time when the water-
  moons splendid
Break with their gold, and are
  scattered or blended
Over the creeks, till the woodlands have warning
Of songs of the bell-bird and wings of the morning.

Welcome as waters unkissed by the summers,
Are the voices of bell-birds to thirsty far-comers.
When fiery December sets foot in the forest,
And the need of the wayfarer presses the sorest,
Pent in the ridges for ever and ever,
The bell-birds direct him to spring and to river,
With ring and with ripple, like runnels whose torrents
Are toned by the pebbles and leaves in the currents.

Often I sit, looking back to a childhood
Mixt with the sights and the sounds of the wildwood,
Longing for power and the sweetness to fashion
Lyrics with beats like the heart-beats of passion—
Songs interwoven of lights and of laughters
Borrowed from bell-birds in far forest-rafters;
So I might keep in the city and alleys
The beauty and strength of the deep mountain valleys,
Charming to slumber the pain of my losses
With glimpses of creeks and a vision of mosses.

Poems of Henry Kendall, 1886

> The first four lines of stanza four were printed in the *Australian Town and Country Journal* on 26 January 1889.

Brumby's Run

Banjo Paterson

[*The Aboriginal term for a wild horse is 'Brumby.'
At a recent trial in Sydney a Supreme Court Judge,
hearing of 'Brumby horses', asked: 'Who is Brumby, and
where is his Run?'*]

It lies beyond the Western Pines
Towards the sinking sun,
And not a survey mark defines
The bounds of 'Brumby's run.'

On odds and ends of mountain land,
On tracks of range and rock,
Where no one else can make a stand,
Old Brumby rears his stock—

A wild, unhandled lot they are
Of every shape and breed.
They venture out 'neath moon and star
Along the flats to feed;

But when the dawn makes pink the sky
And steals along the plain,
The Brumby horses turn and fly
Towards the hills again.

The traveller by the mountain-track
May hear their hoof-beats pass,
And catch a glimpse of brown and black
Dim shadows on the grass.

The eager stockhorse pricks his ears
And lifts his head on high

In wild excitement when he hears
The Brumby mob go by.

Old Brumby asks no price or fee
O'er all his wide domains:
The man who yards his stock is free
To keep them for his pains.

So, off to scour the mountain-side
With eager eyes aglow,
To strongholds where the wild mobs hide
The gully-rakers go.

A rush of horses through the trees,
A red shirt making play;
A sound of stockwhips on the breeze,
They vanish far away!

❖ ❖ ❖

Ah, me! before our day is done
We long with bitter pain
To ride once more on Brumby's run
And yard his mob again.

The Bulletin, 1895

A Bush Christening

Banjo Paterson

On the outer Barcoo where the churches are few,
And men of religion are scanty,
On a road never cross'd 'cept by folk that are lost,
One Michael Magee had a shanty.

Now this Mike was the dad of a ten-year-old lad,
Plump, healthy, and stoutly conditioned;
He was strong as the best, but poor Mike had no rest,
For the youngster had never been christened.

And his wife used to cry, 'if the darlin' should die
Saint Peter would not recognise him.'
But by luck he survived till a preacher arrived,
Who agreed straightaway to baptise him.

Now the artful young rogue, while they held their collogue,
With his ear to the keyhole was listenin',
And he muttered in fright, while his features turned white
'What the divil and all is this christenin'?'

He was none of your dolts, he had seen them brand colts
And it seemed to his small understanding
If the man in the frock made him 'one of the flock'
It must mean something very like branding.

So away with a rush he set off for the brush
While the tears in his eyelids they glistened—
''Tis outrageous,' says he, 'to brand youngsters like me,
I'll be dashed if I'll stop to be christened!'

Like a young native dog he ran into a log
And his father with language uncivil,

A BUSH CHRISTENING

Never heeding the 'praste' cried aloud in his haste
'Come out and be christened, you divil!'

But he lay there as snug as a bug in a rug
And his parents in vain might reprove him,
Till His Reverence spoke (he was fond of a joke)
'I've a notion,' says he, 'that'll move him!'

'Poke a stick up the log, give the spalpeen a prog—
Poke him aisy,—don't hurt him or maim him,
'Tis not long that he'll stand, I've the wather at hand,
As he rushes out this end I'll name him!

Here he comes, and for shame! ye've forgotten the name—
Is it Patsey or Michael or Dinnis?'
Here the youngster ran out, and the priest gave a shout—
'Take your chance, anyhow, wid Maginnis!'

As the howling young cub ran away to the scrub
Where he knew that pursuit would be risky,
The priest, as he fled flung a flask at his head
That was labelled 'MAGINNIS'S WHISKY!'

And Maginnis Magee has been made a J.P.
And the one thing he hates more than sin is
To be asked by the folk, who have heard of the joke,
How he came to be christened 'Maginnis'!

The Bulletin, 1893

A Bush Christmas

CJ Dennis

The sun burns hotly thro' the gums
As down the road old Rogan comes—
   The hatter from the lonely hut
   Beside the track to Woollybutt,
     He likes to spend his Christmas with us here.
He says a man gets sort of strange
Livin' alone without a change,
   Gets sort of settled in his way;
   And so he comes each Christmas day
     To share a bite of tucker and a beer.

Dad and the boys have nought to do,
Except a stray odd job or two.
   Along the fence or in the yard,
   'It ain't a day for workin' hard.'
     Says Dad: 'One day a year don't matter much.'
And then dishevelled, hot and red,
Mum, thro' the doorway puts her head
   And says, 'This Christmas cooking! My!
   The sun's near fit for cooking by.'
     Upon her word she never did see such.

'Your fault,' says Dad, 'you know it is.
Plum puddin'! On a day like this,
   And roasted turkeys! Spare me days!
   I can't get over women's ways.
     In climates such as this the thing's all wrong.
A bit of cold corn-beef an' bread
Would do us very well instead.'
   Then Rogan says, 'You're right; it's hot.
   It makes a feller drink a lot.'
     And Dad gets up and says, 'Well, come along.'

The dinner's served—full bite and sup.
'Come on,' says Mum, 'Now all sit up.'
   The meal takes on a festive air;
   And even father eats his share
      And passes up his plate to have some more.
He laughs and says it's Christmas time,
'That's cookin', Mum. The stuffin's prime.'
   But Rogan pauses once to praise,
   Then eats as tho' he'd starved for days.
      And pitches turkey bones outside the door.

The sun burns hotly thro' the gums,
The chirping of the locusts comes
   Across the paddocks, parched and grey.
   'Whew!' wheezes Father. 'What a day!'
      And sheds his vest. For coats no man had need.
Then Rogan shoves his plate aside
And sighs, as sated men have sighed,
   At many boards in many climes
   On many other Christmas times.
      'By gum!' he says, 'That was a slap-up feed!'

Then, with his black pipe well alight,
Old Rogan brings the kids delight
   By telling o'er again his yarns
   Of Christmas tide 'mid English barns
     When he was, long ago, a farmer's boy.
His old eyes glisten as he sees
Half glimpses of old memories,
   Of whitened fields and winter snows,
   And yuletide logs and mistletoes,
     And all that half-forgotten, hallowed joy.

The children listen, mouths agape,
And see a land with no escape
   For biting cold and snow and frost—
   A land to all earth's brightness lost,
     A strange and freakish Christmas land to them.
But Rogan, with his dim old eyes
Grown far away and strangely wise
   Talks on; and pauses but to ask
   'Ain't there a drop more in that cask?'
     And father nods; but Mother says 'Ahem!'

The sun slants redly thro' the gums
As quietly the evening comes,
   And Rogan gets his old grey mare,
   That matches well his own grey hair,
     And rides away into the setting sun.
'Ah, well,' says Dad. 'I got to say
I never spent a lazier day.
   We ought to get that top fence wired.'
   'My!' sighs poor Mum. 'But I am tired!
     An' all that washing up still to be done.'

The Herald, 1931

The Circus

CJ Dennis

Hey, there! Hoop-la! the circus is in town!
Have you seen the elephant? Have you seen the clown?
Have you seen the dappled horse gallop round the ring?
Have you seen the acrobats on the dizzy swing?
Have you seen the tumbling men tumble up and down?
Hoop-la! Hoop-la! the circus is in town!

Hey, there! Hoop-la! Here's the circus troupe!
Here's the educated dog jumping through the hoop.
See the lady Blondin with the parasol and fan,
The lad upon the ladder and the india-rubber man.
See the joyful juggler and the boy who loops the loop.
Hey! Hey! Hey! Hey! Here's the circus troupe!

A Book for Kids, 1921

Clancy of the Overflow

Banjo Paterson

I had written him a letter which I had, for want of better
Knowledge, sent to where I met him down the Lachlan,
   years ago,
He was shearing when I knew him, so I sent the letter to him,
Just 'on spec,' addressed as follows, 'Clancy, of
   "The Overflow."'

And an answer came directed in a writing unexpected,
(Which I think the same was written with a thumb-nail dipped
   in tar)
'Twas his shearing mate who wrote it, and *verbatim* I will
   quote it:
'Clancy's gone to Queensland droving, and we don't know
   where he are.'

❖ ❖ ❖

In my wild erratic fancy visions come to me of Clancy
Gone a-droving 'down the Cooper' where the Western
   drovers go;
As the stock are slowly stringing, Clancy rides behind them
   singing,
For the drover's life has pleasures that the townsfolk
   never know.

And the bush hath friends to meet him and their kindly voices
   greet him
In the murmur of the breezes and the river on its bars,
And he sees the vision splendid of the sunlit plains extended,
And at night the wond'rous glory of the everlasting stars.

❖ ❖ ❖

I am sitting in my dingy little office, where a stingy
Ray of sunlight struggles feebly down between the houses tall,
And the foetid air and gritty of the dusty, dirty city
Through the open window floating, spreads its foulness
    over all.

And in place of lowing cattle, I can hear the fiendish rattle
Of the tramways and the 'busses making hurry down the street,
And the language uninviting of the gutter children fighting,
Comes fitfully and faintly through the ceaseless tramp of feet.

And the hurrying people daunt me, and their pallid faces
    haunt me
As they shoulder one another in their rush and nervous haste,
With their eager eyes and greedy, and their stunted forms and
    weedy,
For townsfolk have no time to grow, they have no time
    to waste.

And I somehow rather fancy that I'd like to change with
    Clancy,
Like to take a turn at droving where the seasons come and go,
While he faced the round eternal of the cash-book and
    the journal—
But I doubt he'd suit the office, Clancy, of 'The Overflow.'

The Bulletin
(Christmas edition), 1889

The Days of Cobb & Co.

GM Smith (Steele Grey)

We have Telephones and Cables
   And Electric Telegraph,
To flash the news to any point
   In a minute and a half.
To sum it up what way you will,
   It's anything but slow;
It seems a vast improvement
   On the days of Cobb & Co.

We have Electric trams and Cable trams
   The Motor and the Bike;
You can get about the country now
   At any speed you like.
We have railways to the backblocks,
   Where the iron horses go;
And yet the times were better
   In the days of Cobb & Co.

There was enterprise and money,
   And any amount of work;
There was wool and fat stock rolling in
   From the Mitchell Plains and Bourke.
There was merchandise and passengers
   To carry to and fro:
There was life too, in Australia,
   In the days of Cobb & Co.

To travel out a thousand miles
   You'd book yourself in town;
They'd guarantee to pull you through,
   When you paid your money down.
They travelled then by rough bush tracks,
   Through mountains, bog and snow;
And deliver you well up to time
   Would good old Cobb & Co.

They had some splendid drivers,
   Who could handle horses neat,
To see them work their ribbons on
   Those bush tracks was a treat.
And they'd get a change of coaches
   Every twenty miles or so;
And they drove some slashing cattle,
   In the days of Cobb & Co.

Our progress has been rapid,
   But the days are poorer now,
Than the days of Jimmy Tyson, and
   Good old Jacky Dow.
I remember well the sixties,
   And transit then was slow:
But give to me the golden days,
   The days of Cobb & Co.

The Days of Cobb & Co. and other verses, 1906

The Digger's Song

Barcroft Henry Boake

Scrape the bottom of the hole, gather up the stuff,
Fossick in the crannies, lest you leave a grain behind.
Just another shovelful and that'll be enough,
Now we'll take it to the bank and see what we can find,
    Give the dish a twirl around,
    Let the water swirl around,
Gently let it circulate, there's music in the swish,
    And the tinkle of the gravel,
    As the pebbles quickly travel
Around in merry circles on the bottom of the dish.

Ah, if man could only wash his life, if he only could,
Panning off the evil deeds, keeping but the good,
What a mighty lot of digger's dishes would be sold,
Tho' I fear the heap of tailings would be greater than
    the gold,
    Give the dish a twirl around,
    Let the water swirl around,
Man's the sport of circumstance however he may wish,
    Fortune, are you there now?
    Answer to my prayer now,
Drop a half-ounce nugget in the bottom of the dish.

Gently let the water lap, keep the corners dry,
That's about the place the gold'll generally stay,
What was that bright particle that just then caught
    my eye?
I fear me by the look of things 'twas only yellow clay,
    Just another twirl around,
    Let the water swirl around,

That's the way we rob the river of its golden fish,
    What's that? can't we snare a one?
    Don't say that there's ne'er a one,
Bah, there's not a colour in the bottom of the dish!

The Bulletin, 1891

An Exile's Farewell

Adam Lindsay Gordon

The ocean heaves around us still
With long and measured swell,
The autumn gales our canvas fill,
Our ship rides smooth and well.
The broad Atlantic's bed of foam
Still breaks against our prow;
I shed no tears at quitting home,
Nor will I shed them now!

Against the bulwarks on the poop
I lean, and watch the sun
Behind the red horizon stoop—
His race is nearly run.
Those waves will never quench his light,
O'er which they seem to close,
To-morrow he will rise as bright
As he this morning rose.

How brightly gleams the orb of day
Across the trackless sea!
How lightly dance the waves that play
Like dolphins in our lee!
The restless waters seem to say,
In smothered tones to me,
How many thousand miles away
My native land must be!

Speak, Ocean! is my Home the same,
Now all is new to me?—
The tropic sky's resplendent flame,
The vast expanse of sea?

Does all around her, yet unchanged,
The well-known aspect wear?
Oh! can the leagues that I have ranged
Have made no difference there?

How vivid Recollection's hand
Recalls the scene once more!
I see the same tall poplars stand
Beside the garden door;
I see the bird-cage hanging still;
And where my sister set
The flowers in the window-sill—
Can they be living yet?

Let woman's nature cherish grief,
I rarely heave a sigh
Before emotion takes relief
In listless apathy;
While from my pipe the vapours curl
Towards the evening sky,
And 'neath my feet the billows whirl
In dull monotony!

The sky still wears the crimson streak
Of Sol's departing ray,
Some briny drops are on my cheek,
'Tis but the salt sea spray!
Then let our barque the ocean roam,
Our keel the billows plough;
I shed no tears at quitting home,
Nor will I shed them now!

Poems of Adam Lindsay Gordon, 1913

> This version notes that this poem was written 'in a lady's album' by ALG while he was sailing to Australia.

Freedom on the Wallaby

Henry Lawson

Australia's a big country
An' Freedom's humping bluey,
An' Freedom's on the wallaby
Oh! don't you hear 'er cooey?
She's just begun to boomerang,
She'll knock the tyrants silly,
She's goin' to light another fire
And boil another billy.

Our fathers toiled for bitter bread
While loafers thrived beside 'em,
But food to eat and clothes to wear,
Their native land denied 'em.
An' so they left their native land
In spite of their devotion,
An' so they come, or if they stole,
Were sent across the ocean.

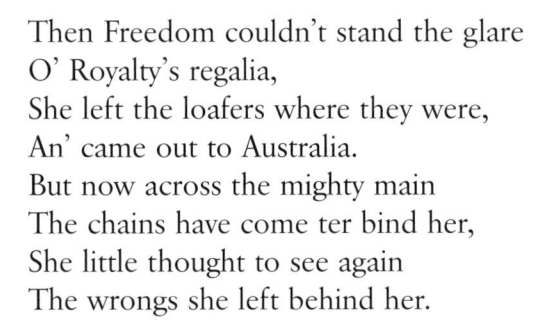

Then Freedom couldn't stand the glare
O' Royalty's regalia,
She left the loafers where they were,
An' came out to Australia.
But now across the mighty main
The chains have come ter bind her,
She little thought to see again
The wrongs she left behind her.

Our parents toiled to make a home,
Hard grubbin' 'twas an' clearin',
They wasn't crowded much with lords
When they was pioneerin'.

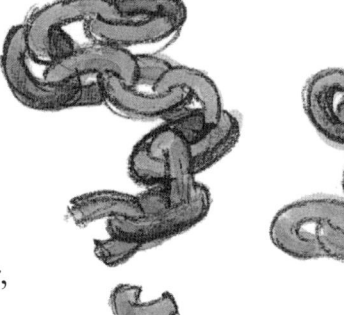

But now that we have made the land
A garden full of promise,
Old Greed must crook 'is dirty hand
And come ter take it from us.

So we must fly a rebel flag,
As others did before us,
And we must sing a rebel song
And join in rebel chorus.
We'll make the tyrants feel the sting
O' those that they would throttle;
They needn't say the fault is ours
If blood should stain the wattle!

The Worker, 1891

> This poem was written for *The Worker*, the monthly official journal of the Federated Workers of Queensland.

Fur and Feathers

Banjo Paterson

The Emus formed a football team
Up Walgett way;
Their dark-brown sweaters were a dream
But kangaroos would sit and scream
To watch them play.

'Now, butterfingers,' they would call,
And such-like names;
The emus couldn't hold the ball
—They had no hands—but hands aren't all
In football games.

A match against the kangaroos
They played one day.
The kangaroos were forced to choose
Some wallabies and wallaroos
That played in grey.

The rules that in the West prevail
Would shock the town;
For when a kangaroo set sail
An emu jumped upon his tail
And fetched him down.

A whistler duck as referee
Was not admired.
He whistled so incessantly
The teams rebelled, and up a tree
He soon retired.

The old marsupial captain said,
'It's do or die!'
So down the ground like fire he fled
And leaped above an emu's head
And scored a try.

Then shouting, 'Keep it on the toes!'
The emus came.
Fierce as the flooded Bogan flows
They laid their foemen out in rows
And saved the game.

On native pear and Darling pea
They dined that night:
But one man was an absentee:
The whistler duck—their referee—
Had taken flight.

The Animals Noah Forgot, 1933

The Geebung Polo Club

Banjo Paterson

It was somewhere up the country, in a land of rock and scrub,
That they formed an institution called the Geebung Polo Club.
They were long and wiry natives from the rugged mountain side,
And the horse was never saddled that the Geebungs couldn't ride;
But their style of playing polo was irregular and rash—
They had mighty little science, but a mighty lot of dash:
And they played on mountain ponies that were muscular and strong,
Though their coats were quite unpolished, and their manes and tails were long.
And they used to train those ponies wheeling cattle in the scrub,
They were demons, were the members of the Geebung Polo Club.

It was somewhere down the country, in a city's smoke and steam,
That a polo club existed, called 'The Cuff and Collar Team'.
As a social institution 'twas a marvellous success,
For the members were distinguished by exclusiveness and dress.
They had natty little ponies that were nice, and smooth, and sleek,
For their cultivated owners only rode 'em once a week.
So they started up the country in pursuit of sport and fame,

For they meant to show the Geebungs how they ought to
 play the game;
And they took their valets with them—just to give their
 boots a rub
Ere they started operations on the Geebung Polo Club.

Now my readers can imagine how the contest ebbed and
 flowed,
When the Geebung boys got going it was time to clear
 the road;
And the game was so terrific that ere half the time
 was gone
A spectator's leg was broken—just from merely looking
 on.
For they waddied one another till the plain was strewn
 with dead,
While the score was kept so even that they neither got
 ahead.
And the Cuff and Collar Captain, when he tumbled off
 to die,
Was the last surviving player—so the game was called
 a tie.

Then the Captain of the Geebungs raised him slowly
 from the ground,
Though his wounds were mostly mortal, yet he fiercely
 gazed around;
There was no one to oppose him—all the rest were in
 a trance,
So he scrambled on his pony for his last expiring chance,
For he meant to make an effort to get victory to his side;
So he struck at goal—and missed it—then he tumbled off
 and died.

❖ ❖ ❖

By the old Campaspe River, where the breezes shake
   the grass,
There's a row of little gravestones that the stockmen
   never pass,
For they bear a crude inscription saying, 'Stranger, drop
   a tear,
For the Cuff and Collar players and the Geebung boys
   lie here.'
And on misty moonlit evenings, while the dingoes howl
   around,
You can see their shadows flitting down that phantom
   polo ground;
You can hear the loud collisions as the flying players meet,
And the rattle of the mallets, and the rush of ponies' feet,
Till the terrified spectator rides like blazes to the pub—
He's been haunted by the spectres of the
   Geebung Polo Club.

The Antipodean, 1893

Going to School

CJ Dennis

Did you see them pass to-day, Billy, Kate and Robin,
All astride upon the back of old grey Dobbin?
Jigging, jogging off to school, down the dusty track—
What must Dobbin think of it—three upon his back?
Robin at the bridle-rein, in the middle Kate,
Billy holding on behind, his legs out straight.

Now they're coming back from school, jig, jog, jig.
See them at the corner where the gums grow big;
Dobbin flicking off the flies and blinking at the sun—
Having three upon his back he thinks is splendid fun:
Robin at the bridle-rein, in the middle Kate,
Little Billy up behind, his legs out straight.

A Book for Kids, 1921

Hist!

CJ Dennis

Hist! .... Hark!
The night is very dark,
And we've to go a mile or so
Across the Possum Park.
Step .... light,
Keeping to the right;
If we delay, and lose our way,
We'll be out half the night.
The clouds are low and gloomy. Oh!
    It's just begun to mist!
    We haven't any overcoats
    And—Hist! .... Hist!

    (Mo .... poke!)
    Who was that that spoke?
    This is not a fitting spot
    To make a silly joke.
    Dear .... me!
  A mopoke in a tree!
 It jarred me so, I didn't know
 Whatever it could be.
But come along; creep along;
Soon we shall be missed.
They'll get a scare and wonder where
We—Hush! .... Hist!

Ssh! .... Soft!
I've told you oft and oft
We should not stray so far away
Without a moon aloft.
Oo! .... Scat!
Goodness! What was that?
Upon my word, it's quite absurd,
It's only just a cat.

But come along; haste along;
Soon we'll have to rush,
Or we'll be late and find the gate
Is—Hist! .... Hush!

 (Kok! .... Korrock!)
  Oh! I've had a shock!
  I hope and trust it's only just
  A frog behind a rock.
  Shoo! .... Shoo!
   We've had enough of you;
   Scaring folk just for a joke
   Is not the thing to do.
  But come along, slip along—
  Isn't it a lark
  Just to roam so far from home
On—Hist! .... Hark!

Look! .... See!
Shining through the tree,
The window-light is glowing
 bright
To welcome you and me.
Shout! .... Shout!
There's someone round about,
And through the door I see some more
And supper all laid out.

Now, run! Run! Run! ...
Oh, we've had such splendid fun—
Through the park in the dark,
As brave as anyone.
Laughed, we did, and chaffed, we did,
And whistled all the way,
And we're home again! Home again!
Hip .... Hooray!

A Book for Kids, 1921

How M'Dougal Topped the Score

Thomas E Spencer

A peaceful spot is Piper's Flat. The folk that live around—
They keep themselves by keeping sheep and turning up
   the ground.
But the climate is erratic; and the consequences are
The struggle with the elements is everlasting war.
We plough, and sow, and harrow—then sit down and pray
   for rain;
And then we get all flooded out and have to start again.
But the folk are now rejoicing as they ne'er rejoiced before,
For we've played Molongo cricket, and M'Dougal topped
   the score!

Molongo had a head on it, and challenged us to play
A single-innings match for lunch—the losing team to pay.
We were not great guns at cricket, but we couldn't well say No,
So we all began to practise, and we let the reaping go.
We scoured the Flat for ten miles round to muster up our men,
But when the list was totalled we could only number ten.
Then up spoke big Tim Brady: he was always slow to speak,
And he said—'What price M'Dougal, who lives down at
   Cooper's Creek?'

So we sent for old M'Dougal, and he stated in reply
That 'he'd never played at cricket, but he'd half a mind to try.
He couldn't come to practice—he was getting in his hay,
But he guessed he'd show the beggars from Molongo how
   to play.'
Now, M'Dougal was a Scotchman, and a canny one at that,
So he started in to practise with a paling for a bat.
He got Mrs. Mac. to bowl him, but she couldn't run at all,

So he trained his sheep-dog, Pincher, how to scout and fetch
   the ball.

Now, Pincher was no puppy; he was old, and worn, and grey;
But he understood M'Dougal, and—accustomed to obey—
When M'Dougal cried out 'Fetch it!' he would fetch it, in
   a trice;
But, until the word was 'Drop it!' he would grip it like a vyce.
And each succeeding night they played until the light grew dim;
Sometimes M'Dougal struck the ball—sometimes the ball struck
   him!
Each time he struck, the ball would plough a furrow in
   the ground,
And when he missed, the impetus would turn him three times
   round.

The fatal day at length arrived—the day that was to see
Molongo bite the dust, or Piper's Flat knocked up a tree!
Molongo's captain won the toss, and sent his men to bat,
And they gave some leather-hunting to the men of Piper's Flat.
When the ball sped where M'Dougal stood, firm planted in
   his track,
He shut his eyes, and turned him round, and stopped it—with
   his *back!*
The highest score was twenty-two, the total sixty-six,
When Brady sent a yorker down that scattered Johnson's sticks.

Then Piper's Flat went in to bat, for glory and renown,
But, like the grass before the scythe, our wickets tumbled
   down.
'Nine wickets down for seventeen, with fifty more to win!'
Our captain heaved a heavy sigh, and sent M'Dougal in.
'Ten pounds to one you lose it!' cried a barracker from town;
But M'Dougal said 'I'll tak' it mon!' and planked the money
   down.

Then he girded up his moleskins in a self-reliant style,
Threw off his hat and boots, and faced the bowler with
  a smile.

He held the bat the wrong side out, and Johnson with a grin,
Stepped lightly to the bowling crease, and sent a 'wobbler' in;
M'Dougal spooned it softly back, and Johnson waited there,
But M'Dougal, cryin' *'Fetch it!'* started running like a hare.
Molongo shouted 'Victory! He's out as sure as eggs.'
When Pincher started through the crowd, and ran through
  Johnson's legs.
He seized the ball like lightning; then he ran behind a log,
And M'Dougal kept on running, while Molongo chased
  the dog.

They chased him up, they chased him down, they chased him
  round, and then
He darted through a slip-rail as the scorer shouted 'Ten!'
M'Dougal puffed; Molongo swore; excitement was intense;
As the scorer marked down twenty, Pincher cleared a barbed-
  wire fence.
'Let us head him!' shrieked Molongo. 'Brain the mongrel with
  a bat!'
'Run it out! Good old McDougal!' yelled the men of Piper's
  Flat.
And McDougal kept on jogging, and then Pincher doubled
  back,
And the scorer counted *'Forty'* as they raced across the track.

McDougal's legs were going fast, Molongo's breath was gone—
But still Molongo chased the dog—McDougal struggled on.
When the scorer shouted *'Fifty!'* then they knew the chase
  would cease;
And McDougal gasped out 'Drop it!' as *he* dropped within
  his crease.
Then Pincher dropped the ball, and as instinctively he knew

HOW M'DOUGAL TOPPED THE SCORE

Discretion was the wiser plan, he disappeared from view.
And as Molongo's beaten men exhausted lay around
We raised McDougal shoulder-high, and bore him from
   the ground.

We bore him to M'Ginniss's, where lunch was ready laid,
And filled him up with whisky-punch, for which Molongo paid.
We drank his health in bumpers, and we cheered him three
   times three,
And when Molongo got its breath, Molongo joined the spree.
And the critics say they never saw a cricket match like that,
When M'Dougal broke the record in the game at Piper's Flat.
And the folks were jubilating as they never were before;
For we played Molongo cricket, and *M'Dougal topped*
   the score!

The Bulletin, 1898

Note the change to McDougal part way through.

The Last of His Tribe

Henry Kendall

He crouches, and buries his face on his knees,
    And hides in the dark of his hair;
For he cannot look up to the storm-smitten trees,
    Or think of the loneliness there—
    Of the loss and the loneliness there.

The wallaroos grope through the tufts of the grass,
    And turn to their coverts for fear;
But he sits in the ashes and lets them pass
    Where the boomerangs sleep with the spear—
    With the nullah, the sling and the spear.

Uloola, behold him! The thunder that breaks
    On the tops of the rocks with the rain,
And the wind which drives up with the salt of the lakes,
    Have made him a hunter again—
    A hunter and fisher again.

For his eyes have been full with a smouldering thought;
    But he dreams of the hunts of yore,
And of foes that he sought, and of fights that he fought
    With those who will battle no more—
    Who will go to the battle no more.

It is well that the water which tumbles and fills,
    Goes moaning and moaning along;
For an echo rolls out from the sides of the hills,
    And he starts at a wonderful song—
    At the sound of a wonderful song.

And he sees, through the rents of the scattering fogs,
 The corroboree warlike and grim,
And the lubra who sat by the fire on the logs,
 To watch, like a mourner, for him—
 Like a mother and mourner for him.

Will he go in his sleep from these desolate lands,
 Like a chief, to the rest of his race,
With the honey-voiced woman who
   beckons and stands,
  And gleams like a dream in
   his face—
  Like a marvellous dream in
   his face?

Poems of Henry Kendall, 1886

The Lights of Cobb and Co.

Henry Lawson

Fire-lighted, on the table a meal for sleepy men,
A lantern in the stable, a jingle now and then;
The mail-coach looming darkly by light of moon and star,
The growl of sleepy voices—a candle in the bar;
A stumble in the passage of folk with wits abroad;
A swear-word from a bedroom—the shout of 'All aboard!'
'Tchk-tchk! Git-up!' 'Hold fast, there!' and down the range we go;
Five hundred miles of scattered camps will watch for Cobb and Co.

Old coaching towns already 'decaying for their sins'
Uncounted Half-Way Houses, and scores of 'Ten Mile Inns';
The riders from the stations by lonely granite peaks;
The black-boy for the shepherds on sheep and cattle creeks;
The roaring camps of Gulgong, and many a 'Digger's Rest';
The diggers on the Lachlan; the huts of Farthest West;
Some twenty thousand exiles who sailed for weal or woe;
The bravest hearts of twenty lands will wait for Cobb and Co.

The morning star has vanished, the frost and fog are gone,
In one of those grand mornings which but on mountains dawn;
A flask of friendly whisky—each other's hopes we share—
And throw our top-coats open to drink the mountain air.
The roads are rare to travel, and life seems all complete;

THE LIGHTS OF COBB AND CO.

The grind of wheels on gravel, the trot of horses' feet,
The trot, trot, trot and canter, as down the spur we go—
The green sweeps to horizons blue that call for Cobb and Co.

We take a bright girl actress through western dust and damps,
To bear the home-world message, and sing for sinful camps,
To wake the hearts and break them, wild hearts that hope and ache—
(Ah! when she thinks of *those* days her own must nearly break!)
Five miles this side the gold-field, a loud, triumphant shout:
Five hundred cheering diggers have snatched the horses out,
With 'Auld Lang Syne' in chorus through roaring camps they go—
That cheer for her, and cheer for Home, and cheer for Cobb and Co.

Three lamps above the ridges and gorges dark and deep,
A flash on sandstone cuttings where sheer the sidings sweep,
A flash on shrouded waggons, on water ghastly white;
Weird bush and scattered remnants of 'rushes' in the night
Across the swollen river a flash beyond the ford:
'Ride hard to warn the driver! He's drunk or mad, good Lord!'
But on the bank to westward a broad, triumphant glow—
A hundred miles shall see to-night the lights of Cobb and Co.!

Swift scramble up the siding where teams climb inch
    by inch;
Pause, bird-like, on the summit—then breakneck down
    the 'pinch'!
Past haunted half-way houses—where convicts made
    the bricks—
Scrub-yards and new bark shanties, we dash with five
    and six—
By clear, ridge-country rivers, and gaps where tracks
    run high,
Where waits the lonely horseman, cut clear against
    the sky;
Through stringy-bark and blue-gum, and box and pine
    we go;
New camps are stretching 'cross the plains the routes of
    Cobb and Co.

Throw down the reins, old driver—there's no one left to
    shout;
The ruined inn's survivor must take the horses out.
A poor old coach hereafter!—we're lost to all such things—
No bursts of songs or laughter shall shake your leathern
    springs.
When creeping in unnoticed by railway sidings drear,
Or left in yards for lumber, decaying with the year—
Oh, who'll think how in those days when distant fields
    were broad
You raced across the Lachlan side with twenty-five on
    board.

Not all the ships that sail away since Roaring Days are
    done—
Not all the boats that steam from port, nor all the trains
    that run,

Shall take such hopes and loyal hearts—for men shall never know
Such days as when the Royal Mail was run by Cobb and Co.
The 'greyhounds' race across the sea, the 'special' cleaves the haze,
But these seem dull and slow compared with bygone Roaring Days!
The eyes that watched are dim with age, and souls are weak and slow,
The hearts are dust or hardened now that broke for Cobb and Co.

The Bulletin (Christmas edition), 1897

The Man from Ironbark

Banjo Paterson

It was the man from Ironbark who struck the Sydney town,
He wandered over street and park he wandered up and down.
He loitered here, he loitered there, till he was like to drop
Until at last in sheer despair he sought a barber's shop.
''Ere! shave my hair and whiskers off, I'll be a man of mark,
I'll go and do the Sydney toff up home in Ironbark.'

The barber man was small and flash, as barbers mostly are,
He wore a strike-your-fancy sash, he smoked a huge cigar:
He was a humorist of note and keen at repartee,
He laid the odds and kept a 'tote' whatever that may be,
And when he saw our friend arrive he whispered 'here's a lark!
Just watch me catch him all alive, this man from Ironbark.'

There were some gilded youths that sat along the barber's wall,
Their eyes were dull, their heads were flat, they had no brains
   at all;
To them the barber passed the wink, his dexter eyelid shut,
'I'll make this bloomin' yokel think his bloomin' throat is cut.'
And as he soaped and rubbed it in he made a rude remark:
'I s'pose the flats is pretty green up there in Ironbark.'

A grunt was all reply he got; he shaved the bushman's chin,
Then made the water boiling hot and dipped the razor in.
He raised his hand, his brow grew black, he paused awhile
   to gloat,
Then slashed the red-hot razor-back across his victim's throat;
Upon the newly shaven skin it made a livid mark—
No doubt it fairly took him in the man from Ironbark.

He fetched a wild up-country yell the dead might wake to hear,
And though his throat, he knew full well was cut from ear to ear,

He struggled gamely to his feet, and faced the murd'rous foe
'You've done for me! you dog, I'm beat! One hit before I go!
I only wish I had a knife, you blessed murdering shark!
But you'll remember all your life, the man from Ironbark.'

He lifted up his hairy paw, with one tremendous clout
He landed on the barber's jaw, and knocked the barber out.
He set to work with tooth and nail, he made the place a wreck;
He grabbed the nearest gilded youth and tried to break
   his neck.
And all the while his throat he held to save his vital spark,
And 'Murder! Bloody Murder!' yelled the man from Ironbark.

A peeler man who heard the din came in to see the show,
He tried to run the bushman in, but he refused to go.
And when at last the barber spoke, and said, ''twas all in fun,
'Twas just a little harmless joke, a trifle overdone.'
'A joke!' he cried, 'by George, that's fine, a lively sort of lark;
I'd like to catch that murdering swine some night in Ironbark.'

And now while round the shearing floor the list'ning shearers
   gape,
He tells the story o'er and o'er and brags of his escape.
'Them barber chaps what keeps a tote, by George, I've had
   enough,
One tried to cut my bloomin' throat, but thank the Lord it's
   tough!'
And whether he's believed or no, there's
   one thing to remark,
That flowing beards are all the go way up in
   Ironbark.

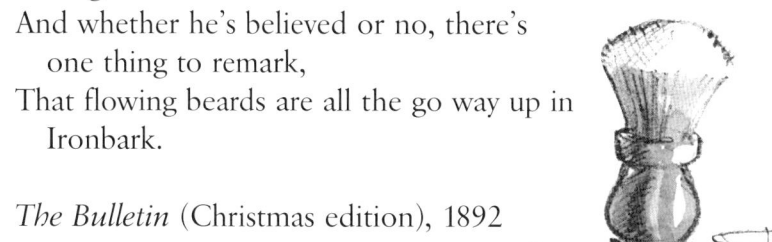

The Bulletin (Christmas edition), 1892

The Man from Snowy River

Banjo Paterson

There was movement at the station, for the word had
    passed around
That the colt from old Regret had got away
And had joined the wild bush horses—he was worth a
    thousand pound—
So all the cracks had gathered to the fray.
All the tried and noted riders from the stations near
    and far
Had mustered at the homestead over-night,
For the bushmen love hard-riding where the fleet wild
    horses are,
And the stockhorse snuffs the battle with delight.

There was Harrison, who made his pile when Pardon
    won the Cup,
The old man with his hair as white as snow,
But few could ride beside him when his blood was fairly
    up—
He would go wherever horse and man could go.
And Clancy of the Overflow came down to lend a hand—
No better horseman ever held the reins;
For never horse could throw him while the saddle-girths
    would stand,
He learnt to ride while droving on the plains.

And one was there, a stripling on a small and graceful
    beast;
He was something like a racehorse undersized,
With a touch of Timor pony, three parts thoroughbred
    at least,
The sort that are by mountain horsemen prized.

He was hard and tough and wiry—just the sort that won't
   say die;
There was courage in his quick impatient tread,
And he bore the badge of gameness in his bright and
   fiery eye,
And the proud and lofty carriage of his head.

But still so slight and weedy one would doubt his power
   to stay,
And the old man said, 'That horse will never do
For a long and tiring gallop—lad, you'd better stop away,
The hills are far too rough for such as you.'
So he waited sad and wistful; only Clancy stood his
   friend.
'I think we ought to let him come,' he said;
'I warrant he'll be with us when he's wanted at the end,
For both his horse and he are mountain bred.
'He hails from Snowy River, up by Kosciusko's side,
Where the hills are twice as steep and twice as rough—
Where a horse's hoofs strike firelight from the flint stones
   every stride,
The man that holds his own is good enough.
And the Snowy River riders on the mountains make
   their home,
Where the river runs those giant hills between.
I have seen full many horsemen since I first commenced
   to roam,
But never yet such horsemen have I seen.'

So he went; they found the horses by the big Mimosa
   clump;
They raced away towards the mountain's brow,
And the old man gave his orders, 'Boys, go at them from
   the jump,
No use to try for fancy-riding now;

And, Clancy, you must wheel them—try and wheel them
   to the right.
Ride boldly, lad, and never fear the spills,
For never yet was rider that could keep the mob in sight,
If once they gain the shelter of those hills.'

So Clancy rode to wheel them—he was racing on the wing
Where the best and boldest riders take their place—
And he raced his stock-horse past them, and he made the
   ranges ring
With the stockwhip, as he met them face to face,
And they wavered for a moment while he swung the
   dreaded lash,
But they saw their well-loved mountain full in view,
And they charged beneath the stockwhip with a sharp
   and sudden dash,
And off into the mountain-scrub they flew.

Then fast the horsemen followed where the gorges deep
   and black
Resounded to the thunder of their tread,
And the stockwhips woke the echoes, and they fiercely
   answered back
From cliffs and crags that beetled overhead;
And upward, upward ever, the wild horses held their way
Where mountain-ash and kurrajong grew wide.
And the old man muttered fiercely: 'We may bid the mob
   good-day,
No man can hold them down the other side.'

When they reached the mountain's summit even Clancy
   took a pull—
It well might make the boldest hold their breath,
The wild hop-scrub grew thickly and the hidden ground
   was full
Of wombat-holes, and any slip was death;

THE MAN FROM SNOWY RIVER

But the man from Snowy River let his pony have his head,
And he swung his stockwhip round and gave a cheer,
And he raced him down the mountain like a torrent
   down its bed,
While the others stood and watched in very fear.

He sent the flint-stones flying, but the pony kept his feet;
He cleared the fallen timber in his stride,
And the man from Snowy River never shifted in his seat—

It was grand to see that mountain horseman ride
Through stringy barks and saplings on the rough and
   broken ground,
Down the hillside at a racing-pace he went,
And he never drew the bridle till he landed safe and
   sound
At the bottom of that terrible descent.

He was right among the horses as they climbed the
   further hill,
And the watchers, on the mountain standing mute,
Saw him ply the stockwhip fiercely—he was right among
   them still
As he raced across the clearing in pursuit;
Then they lost him for a moment where the mountain
   gullies met
In the ranges—but a final glimpse reveals
On a dim and distant hillside the wild horses racing yet
With the man from Snowy River at their heels.

And he ran them single-handed till their sides were white
   with foam.
He followed like a bloodhound on their track
Till they halted, cowed and beaten—then he turned their
   heads for home,
And alone and unassisted brought them back;
And his hardy mountain pony—he could scarcely raise
   a trot—
He was blood from hip to shoulder from the spur,
But his pluck was still undaunted and his courage
   fiery hot,
For never yet was mountain horse a cur.

And down by Araluen, where the stony ridges raise
Their torn and rugged battlements on high,
Where the air is clear as crystal and the white stars
   fairly blaze
At midnight in the cold and frosty sky,
And where, around 'the Overflow,' the reedbeds sweep
   and sway
To the breezes and the rolling plains are wide,
The man from Snowy River is a household word to-day,
And the stockmen tell the story of his ride.

The Bulletin, 1890

> Have a close look at the front of the current Australian $10 note. Can you see:
> - an extract from this poem written in Paterson's own handwriting?
> - an illustration inspired by this poem? It was based on lithographs and photographs printed in 1870s newspapers.
>
> In the last verse there is often a different first line:
> *And down by Araluen, where the stony ridges raise*
> becomes
> *And down by Kosciusko, where the pine-clad ridges raise*

Mr Smith

DH Souter

MR SMITH OF TALLABUNG
HAS VERY WICKED WAYS,
HE WANDERS OFF INTO THE BUSH
AND STAYS AWAY FOR DAYS

He never says he's going;
We only know he's gone.
There's lots of cats like Mr Smith,
Who like to walk alone.

He plays that he's a tiger,
And makes the dingoes run.
He scratches emus on the legs
And plays at football with their eggs;
But does it all in fun.

And then one day, he's home again,
The skin all off his nose;
His ears all torn and tattered,
His face all bruised and battered,
And bindies in his toes.

He wanders round and finds a place
To sleep in in the sun.
And dream of all the wicked things
That he has been and done.

MR SMITH OF TALLABUNG
MAY BE A BAD CAT;
BUT EVERYBODY LIKES HIM—
SO THAT'S JUST THAT.

Bush-Babs: with pictures, 1933

> *Bush-Babs:* with pictures is Souter's collection of nursery rhymes (Souter called them jingles), some of which he wrote and illustrated for his children. It was published in 1933. The 'Souter cat' is there along with a sketch of DH Souter himself in the introduction. Cats also feature on chairs he owned, in sketches and on his chinaware.

Mulga Bill's Bicycle

Banjo Paterson

'Twas Mulga Bill, from Eaglehawk, that caught the cycling craze.
He turned away the good old horse that served him many days.
He dressed himself in cycling clothes, resplendent to be seen.
He hurried off to town and bought a shining new machine;
And as he wheeled it through the door, with air of lordly pride,
The grinning shop assistant said, 'Excuse me, can you ride?'

'See here, young man,' said Mulga Bill, 'from Walgett to the sea,
From Conroy's Gap to Castlereagh, there's none can ride like me.
I'm good all round at everything, as everybody knows,
Although I'm not the one to talk—I *hate* a man that blows.

'But riding is my special gift, my chiefest, sole delight;
Just ask a wild duck can it swim, a wild cat can it fight.
There's nothing clothed in hair or hide, or built of flesh or steel,
There's nothing walks or jumps, or runs, on axle, hoof, or wheel,
But what I'll sit, while hide will hold and girths and straps are tight.
I'll ride this here two-wheeled concern right straight away at sight.'

'Twas Mulga Bill, from Eaglehawk, that sought his own abode,
That perched above the Dead Man's Creek, beside the mountain road.
He turned the cycle down the hill and mounted for the fray,
But ere he'd gone a dozen yards it bolted clean away.

It left the track, and through the trees, just like a silver streak,
It whistled down the awful slope towards the Dead Man's Creek.

It shaved a stump by half an inch, it dodged a big white-box:
The very wallaroos in fright went scrambling up the rocks,
The wombats hiding in their caves dug deeper underground,
As Mulga Bill, as white as chalk, sat tight to every bound.
It struck a stone and gave a spring that cleared a fallen tree.
It raced beside a precipice as close as close could be;
And then as Mulga Bill let out one last despairing shriek
It made a leap of 20 feet into the Dead Man's Creek.

'Twas Mulga Bill, from Eaglehawk, that slowly swam ashore:
He said, 'I've had some narrer shaves and lively rides before;
I've rode a wild bull round a yard to win a five-pound bet,
But this was the most awful ride that I've encountered yet.
I'll give that two-wheeled outlaw best; it's shaken all my nerve
To feel it whistle through the air and plunge and buck and swerve
It's safe at rest in Dead Man's Creek, we'll leave it lying still;
A horse's back is good enough henceforth for Mulga Bill.'

The Sydney Mail, 1896

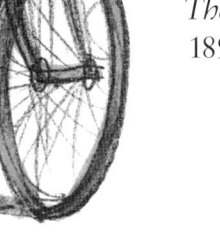

My Typewriter

Edward Dyson

I have a trim typewriter now,
They tell me none is better;
It makes a pleasing, rhythmic row,
And neat is every letter.
I tick out stories by machine,
Dig pars, and gags, and verses keen,
And lathe them off in manner slick.
It is so easy, and it's quick.

And yet it falls short, I'm afraid,
Of giving satisfaction,
This making literature by aid
Of scientific traction;
For often, I can't fail to see,
The dashed thing runs
   away with me.
It bolts, and do whate'er
   I may
I cannot hold the
   runaway.

It is not fitted with a
   brake,
And endless are my verses,
Nor any yarn I start to make
Appropriately terse is.
'Tis plain that this machine-made screed
Is fit but for machines to read;
So 'Wanted' (as an iron censor)
'A good, sound, secondhand condenser!'

The Bulletin, 1917

Native Companions Dancing

John Shaw Neilson

On the blue plains in wintry days
These stately birds move in the dance.
Keen eyes have they, and quaint old ways
On the blue plains in wintry days.
The Wind, their unseen Piper, plays,
They strut, salute, retreat, advance;
On the blue plains, in wintry days,
These stately birds move in the dance.

*Collected Poems of
John Shaw Neilson*, 1934

Old Granny Sullivan

John Shaw Neilson

A pleasant shady place it is, a pleasant place and cool—
The township folk go up and down, the children pass
   to school.
Along the river lies my world, a dear sweet world to me:
I sit and learn—I cannot go; there is so much to see.

But Granny, she has seen the world, and often by her side
I sit and listen while she speaks of youthful days of pride;
Old Granny's hands are clasped; she wears her favourite
   faded shawl—
I ask her this, I ask her that: she says, 'I mind them all.'

The boys and girls that Granny knew, far o'er the seas
   are they;
But there's no love like the old love, and the old world
   far away;
Her talk is all of wakes and fairs—or how, when night
   would fall,
'Twas many a quare thing crept and came!' and Granny
   'minds them all.'

A strange new land was this to her, and perilous, rude
   and wild—
Where loneliness and tears and care came to each
   mother's child:
The wilderness closed all around, grim as a prison wall;
But white folk then were stout of heart—ah! Granny
   'minds it all.'

The day she first met Sullivan—she tells it all to me—
How she was hardly twenty-one, and he was twenty-three.
The courting days! the kissing days!—but bitter things
    befall
The bravest hearts that plan and dream. Old Granny
    'minds it all.'

Her wedding-dress I know by heart: yes! every flounce
    and frill;
And the little home they lived in first, with the garden on
    the hill.
'Twas there her baby boy was born, and neighbours came
    to call,
But none had seen a boy like Jim—and Granny 'minds
    it all.'

They had their fight in those old days; but Sullivan was
    strong,
A smart quick man at anything; 'Twas hard to put him
    wrong . . .
One day they brought him from the mine . . . (The big
    salt tears will fall) . . .
''Twas long ago, God rest his soul!' Poor Granny 'minds
    it all.'

The first dark days of widowhood, the weary days and
    slow,
The grim, disheartening, uphill fight, then Granny lived
    to know.
'The childer,' ah! they grew and grew—sound, rosy-
    cheeked, and tall:
'The childer' still they are to her. Old Granny 'minds
    them all.'

How well she loved her little brood! Oh, Granny's heart was brave!
She gave to them her love and faith—all that the good God gave.

They change not with the changing years: as babies just
   the same
She feels for them—though some, alas, have brought her
   grief and shame.

The big world called them here and there, and many a
   mile away:
They cannot come—she cannot go—the darkness haunts
   the day;
And I, no flesh and blood of hers, sit here while shadows
   fall—
I sit and listen—Granny talks; for Granny 'minds them all.'

Just fancy Granny Sullivan at seventeen or so,
In all the floating finery that women love to show;
And oh! It is a merry dance: the fiddler's flushed
   with wine
And Granny's partner brave and gay, and Granny's eyes
   ashine . . .*

'Tis time to pause, for pause we must: we only have
   our day:
Yes: by and by our dance will die, our fiddlers cease
   to play;
And we shall seek some quiet place where great grey
   shadows fall,
And sit and wait as Granny waits—we'll sit and 'mind
   them all.'

The Bookfellow, 1907

* *This stanza is not included in his published volume of
poetry,* Collected Poems of John Shaw Neilson.

Old Man Platypus

Banjo Paterson

Far from the trouble and toil of town,
Where the reed beds sweep and shiver,
Look at a fragment of velvet brown—
Old Man Platypus drifting down,
Drifting along the river.

And he plays and dives in the river bends
In a style that is most elusive;
With few relations and fewer friends,
For Old Man Platypus descends
From a family most exclusive.

He shares his burrow beneath the bank
With his wife and his son and daughter
At the roots of the reeds and the grasses rank;
And the bubbles show where our hero sank
To its entrance under water.

Safe in their burrow below the falls
They live in a world of wonder,
Where no one visits and no one calls,
They sleep like little brown billiard balls
With their beaks tucked neatly under.

And he talks in a deep unfriendly growl
As he goes on his journey lonely;
For he's no relation to fish nor fowl,
Nor to bird nor beast, nor to horned owl;
In fact, he's the one and only!

The Animals Noah Forgot, 1933

On the Night Train

Henry Lawson

Have you seen the bush by moonlight, from the train, go running by?
Blackened log and stump and sapling, ghostly trees all dead and dry;
Here a patch of glassy water; there a glimpse of mystic sky?
Have you heard the still voice calling—yet so warm, and yet so cold:—
'I'm the Mother-Bush that bore you! Come to me when you are old'?

Did you see the Bush below you sweeping darkly to the range,
All unchanged and all unchanging, yet so very old and strange!
While you thought in softened anger of the things that did estrange?—
(Did you hear the Bush a-calling, when your heart was young and bold:—
'I'm the Mother-bush that nursed you; Come to me when you are old'?)
In the cutting or the tunnel, out of sight of stock or shed,
Did you hear the grey Bush calling from the pine-ridge overhead:—
'You have seen the seas and cities—all is cold to you, or dead—
All seems done and all seems told, but the grey-light turns to gold!
I'm the Mother-Bush that loves you—Come to me now you are old'?

Birth, A Little Journal of
Australian Poetry, 1922

'Ough!'

WT Goodge

(A fonetic fansy, dedicated to Androo Karnegee, the millionaire spelling reformer.)

The baker-man was kneading dough
And whistling softly, sweet and lough.

Yet ever and anon he'd cough
As though his head were coming ough!

'My word!' said he, 'but this is rough;
This flour is simply awful stough!'

He punched and thumped it through and through,
As all good bakers always dough!

'I'd sooner drive,' said he, 'a plough
Than be a baker, anyhough!'

Thus spake the baker
   kneading dough;
But don't let on I told
   you sough!

The Bulletin, 1906

The Pieman

CJ Dennis

I'd like to be a pieman, and ring a little bell,
Calling out, 'Hot pies! Hot pies to sell!'
Apple-pies and Meat-pies, Cherry-pies as well,
Lots and lots and lots of pies—more than you can tell.
Big, rich Pork-pies! Oh, the lovely smell!
   But I wouldn't be a pie-man if . . .
      I wasn't very well.
         Would you?

A Book for Kids, 1921

Pioneers

Frank Hudson

We are the old-world people,
Ours were the hearts to dare;
But our youth is spent, and our backs are bent,
And the snow is on our hair.

Back in the early fifties,
Dim through the mist of years,
By the bush-grown strand of
   a wild strange land
We entered—the Pioneers.

Our axes rang in the
   woodlands,
Where the gaudy bush-birds flew,
And we turned the loam of our new-found home,
Where the eucalyptus grew.

Housed in the rough log shanty,
Camped in the leaking tent,
From sea to view of the mountains blue,
Where the eager fossickers went.

We wrought with a will unceasing,
We moulded, and fashioned, and planned,
And we fought with the black, and we blazed the track,
That ye might inherit the land.

Here are your shops and churches,
Your cities of stucco and smoke;
And the swift trains fly, where the wild-cat's cry
Once the sad bush silence broke.

Take now the fruit of our labour,
Nourish and guard it with care,
For our youth is spent, and our backs are bent.
And the snow is on our hair.

The Song of Manly Men and other verses, 1908

Pioneers

Banjo Paterson

They came of bold and roving stock that would not fixed abide;
They were the sons of field and flock since e'er they learnt to ride,
We may not hope to see such men in these degenerate years
As those explorers of the bush—the brave old pioneers.

'Twas they that rode the trackless bush in heat and storm and drought;
'Twas they that heard the master-word that called them farther out;
'Twas they that followed up the trail the mountain cattle made,
And pressed across the mighty range where now their bones are laid.

But now the times are dull and slow, the brave old days are dead
When hardy bushmen started out, and forced their way ahead
By tangled scrub and forests grim towards the unknown west,
And spied the far-off promised land from off the ranges' crest.

Oh! ye, that sleep in lonely graves by far-off ridge and plain,
We drink to you in silence now as Christmas comes again,
The men who fought the wilderness through rough unsettled years—
The founders of our nation's life, the brave old pioneers.

Australian Town and Country Journal, 1896

Pitchin' at the Church

PJ Hartigan (John O'Brien)

On the Sunday morning mustered,
Yarning at our ease;
Buggies, traps and jinkers clustered
Underneath the trees,
Horses tethered to the fences;
Thus we hold our conferences
Waiting till the priest commences—
Pitchin' at the Church.

Sheltering in the summer's shining
Where the shadows fall;
When the winter's sun is pining,
Lined along the wall;
Yarning, reckoning, ruminating,
'Yeos' and lambs and wool debating,
Squatting, smoking, idly waiting—
Pitchin' at the Church.

Young bloods gathered from the others
Tell their dreamings o'er;
Beaded-bonneted old mothers
Grouped around the door;
Dainty bush girls, trim and fairy,
All that's neat and sweet and airy—
Nell, and Kate, and Laughing Mary—
Pitchin' at the Church.

Up comes someone briskly driving,
'Cutting matters fine':
All his 'fam'ly lot' arriving
Wander in a line
Off in some precise direction,

PITCHIN' AT THE CHURCH

Till they find their proper section,
Greet it with an interjection—
Pitchin' at the Church.

'Mornun', Jack.' 'Good-mornun', Martin.'
'Keepin' pretty dry!'
'When d'you think you'll finish cartin'?'
'Prices ain't too high?'
Round about the yarnin' strayin'—
Dances, sickness—frocks surveyin'—
Wheat is 'growed,' the 'hens is layin''—
Pitchin' at the Church.

*Around the Boree Log and
other verses, 1922*

Poets

CJ Dennis

Each poet that I know (he said)
Has something funny in his head,
   Some wandering growth or queer disease
   That gives to him a strange unease.
If such a thing he hasn't got
What makes him write his silly rot?
   All poets' brains, so I have found,
   Go, like the music, round and round.

Why they are suffered e'er to tread
This sane man's earth seems strange (he said).
   I've never met a poet yet,
   A rhymster I have never met
Who could talk sense like any man—
Like I, or even you, say, can.
   They make me sick! The time seems ripe
   To clean them up and all their tripe.

And yet (He stopped and felt his head)
I met a poet once (he said)
   Who, when I said he made me sick
   Hit me a punch like a mule's kick.
That only goes to prove again
The theory that I maintain:
   A man who can't gauge that crazy bunch;
   No poet ought to pack a punch.

Of all the poetry I've read
I've never yet seen one (he said)
   That couldn't be, far as it goes,
   Much better written out in prose.

It's what they eat, I often think;
Or, yet more likely, what they drink.
   Aw, poets! All the tribe, by heck,
   Give me a swift pain in the neck.

The Herald, 1936

Post-Hole Mick

GM Smith (Steele Grey)

A short time back while over in Vic.
I met with a chap called Post-Hole Mick;
He was a raw-boned, loose-built son of a paddy
And at putting down post-holes he was the daddy.

And wherever you'd meet him, near or far,
He had always his long-handled shovel and bar,
I suppose you all know what I mean by a bar,
It's a lump of wrought-iron the shape of a spar.

With one chisel end for digging the ground
And average weight about twenty pound;
Mick worked for the cockies around Geelong,
For a time they kept him going strong.

He would sink them a hundred holes for a bob,
And, of course, soon worked himself out of a job.
But when post-hole sinking got scarce for Mick,
He greased his brogues and cut his stick.

And one fine day he left Geelong
And took his shovel and bar along.
He took to the track in search of work,
And struck due north, enroute to Bourke.

It seems he had been some time on tramp
When one day he struck a fencers' camp.
The contractor there was wanting a hand,
As post-hole sinkers were in demand.

POST-HOLE MICK

He showed him the line and put him on,
But while he looked round, shure Mick was gone.
There were the holes, but where was the man?
Then his eye along the line he ran.

He'd already put down about ninety-nine,
And at the rate of a hunt he was running the line.
He had a few sinkers he thought was quick
Till the day he engaged with Post-Hole Mick.

When he finished his contract he started forth,
And it appears kept on his course due north;
For I saw a report in the Croydon Star
Where a fellow had passed with a shovel and bar.

To give you an idea of how he could walk
A day or two later he struck Cape York.
If they can't find him work there
putting down holes
I'm afraid he'll arrive at one of
the poles.

*The Days of Cobb & Co.
and other verses*, 1906

The Roaring Days

Henry Lawson

The night too quickly passes
And we are growing old,
So let us fill our glasses
And toast the Days of Gold:
When finds of wond'rous treasure
Set all the South ablaze,
And you and I were faithful mates
All through the roarin' days!

Then stately ships came sailing
From ev'ry harbour's mouth,
And sought the land of promise
That beaconed in the South;
Then southward streamed their streamers
And swelled their canvas full
To speed the wildest dreamers
E'er borne in vessel's hull!

And 'neath the sunny dadoes,
Against the lower skies,
The shining Eldoradoes,
Forever would arise;
And all the bush awakened,
Was stirred in wild unrest,
And all the year a human stream
Went pouring to the West. **

The rough bush roads re-echoed
The bar-room's noisy din,
When troops of stalwart horsemen
Dismounted at the inn.
And oft the hearty greetings

And hearty clasp of hands,
Would tell of sudden meetings
Of friends from other lands;
When, puzzled long, the new-chum
Would recognise at last,
Behind a bronzed and bearded skin,
A comrade of the past.

And when the cheery camp-fire
Suffused the bush with gleams,
The camping-grounds were crowded
With caravans of teams;
Then home the jests were driven,
And good old songs were sung,
And choruses were given,
The strength of heart and lung.
Oh, they were lion-hearted
Who gave our country birth!
Oh, they were of the stoutest sons
From all the lands on earth!

Oft when the camps were dreaming,
And fires began to pale,
Then thro' the ranges gleaming
Would come the Royal Mail.
Then, drawn by foaming horses,
And lit by flashing lamps,
Old 'Cobb and Co.'s,' in Royal State,
Went dashing past the camps.

Oh, who would paint a gold-field,
And limn the scene aright,
As we have often seen it
In early morning's light;
The yellow mounds of mullock
With spots of red and white,

The scattered quartz that glistened
Like diamonds in light;
The azure line of ridges,
The bush of darkest green,
The little homes of calico
That dotted all the scene.

I hear the fall of timber
From distant flats and fells,
The pealing of the anvils
As clear as little bells,
The rattle of the cradle,
The clack of windlass-boles,
The flutter of the crimson flags
Above the golden holes.

❖ ❖ ❖

Ah, then our hearts were bolder,
And if our fortune frowned
Our swags we'd lightly shoulder
And tramp to other ground.
But golden days are vanished,
And altered is the scene;
The diggings are deserted
The camping-grounds are green.
The flaunting flag of progress
Is in the West unfurled,
The mighty bush with iron rails
Is tethered to the world.

** *alternative verse*

Their shining Eldorado,
Beneath the southern skies,
Was day and night for ever
Before their eager eyes.
The brooding bush, awakened,
Was stirred in wild unrest,
And all the year a human stream
Went pouring to the West.

The Bulletin (Christmas edition), 1889

A Ruined Reversolet

CJ Dennis

'Tis Spring!
Sing Hey!
Birds sing
All day.
In trees
Bees hum—
I' sneeze—
Skatch-Humb!!
I sdeeze.
Bees hub.
Id trees
All day
Birds sig.
Sig Hey!
'Tis Sprig!

The Bulletin, 1908

A RUINED REVERSOLET

Said Hanrahan

PJ Hartigan (John O'Brien)

'We'll all be rooned,' said Hanrahan,
In accents most forlorn,
Outside the church, ere Mass began,
One frosty Sunday morn.

The congregation stood about,
Coat-collars to the ears,
And talked of stock, and crops, and drought,
As it had done for years.

'It's lookin' crook,' said Daniel Croke;
'Bedad, it's cruke, me lad,
For never since the banks went broke
Has seasons been so bad.'

'It's dry, all right,' said young O'Neil,
With which astute remark
He squatted down upon his heel
And chewed a piece of bark.

And so around the chorus ran
'It's keepin' dry, no doubt.'
'We'll all be rooned,' said Hanrahan,
'Before the year is out.'

'The crops are done; ye'll have your work
To save one bag of grain;
From here way out to Back-o'-Bourke
They're singin' out for rain.

'They're singin' out for rain,' he said,
'And all the tanks are dry.'
The congregation scratched its head,
And gazed around the sky.

'There won't be grass, in any case,
Enough to feed an ass;
There's not a blade on Casey's place
As I came down to Mass.'

'If rain don't come this month,' said Dan,
And cleared his throat to speak—
'We'll all be rooned,' said Hanrahan,
'If rain don't come this week.'

A heavy silence seemed to steal
On all at this remark;
And each man squatted on his heel,
And chewed a piece of bark.

'We want a inch of rain, we do,'
O'Neil observed at last;
But Croke 'maintained' we wanted two
To put the danger past.

'If we don't get three inches, man,
Or four to break this drought,
We'll all be rooned,' said Hanrahan,
'Before the year is out.'

In God's good time down came the rain;
And all the afternoon
On iron roof and window-pane
It drummed a homely tune.

And through the night it pattered still,
And lightsome, gladsome elves
On dripping spout and window-sill
Kept talking to themselves.

It pelted, pelted all day long,
A-singing at its work,
Till every heart took up the song
Way out to Back-o'-Bourke.

And every creek a banker ran,
And dams filled overtop;
'We'll all be rooned,' said Hanrahan,
'If this rain doesn't stop.'

And stop it did, in God's good time:
And spring came in to fold
A mantle o'er the hills sublime
Of green and pink and gold.

And days went by on dancing feet,
With harvest-hopes immense,
And laughing eyes beheld the wheat
Nid-nodding o'er the fence.

And, oh, the smiles on every face,
As happy lad and lass
Through grass knee-deep on Casey's place
Went riding down to Mass.

While round the church in clothes genteel
Discoursed the men of mark,
And each man squatted on his heel,
And chewed his piece of bark,

'There'll be bush-fires for sure, me man,
There will, without a doubt;
We'll all be rooned,' said Hanrahan,
'Before the year is out.'

Around the Boree Log and other verses, 1922

In 1911 PJ Hartigan (John O'Brien) purchased his first motor car. He was one of the first curates in NSW to own one. He loved cars. During his life he owned many! Father O'Brien was once asked by the Albury parish priest to drive him to administer the last rites to a man called Jack Riley. After receiving the last rites, Father O'Brien recited 'The Man from Snowy River' not knowing that Riley had told Banjo Paterson about one of his rides, the ride that became Paterson's famous poem.

Santa Claus in the Bush

Banjo Paterson

It chanced out back at the Christmas time,
When the wheat was ripe and tall,
A stranger rode to the farmer's gate—
A sturdy man, and a small.

'Run down, run down, my little son Jack,
And bid the stranger stay;
And we'll hae a crack for the "Auld Lang Syne,"
For to-morrow is Christmas Day.'

'Nay now, nay now,' said the dour gude wife,
'But ye should let him be;
He's maybe only a drover chap
From the land o' the Darling Pea.

'Wi' a drover's tales, and a drover's thirst
To swiggle the hail night through;
Or he's maybe a life assurance carle,
To talk ye black and blue.'

'Gude wife, he's never a drover chap,
For their swags are neat and thin;
And he's never a life assurance carle,
Wi' the brick-dust burnt in his skin.

'Gude wife, gude wife, be not so dour,
For the wheat stands ripe and tall,
And we shore wi' a seven-pound fleece this year,
Ewes and weaners and all.

'There is grass to spare, and the stock are fat.
When the whiles are gaunt and thin,
And we owe a tithe to the travelling poor,
So we must ask him in.

'You can set him a chair to the table side,
And give him a bite to eat;
An omelette made of a new laid egg,
Or a tasty bit of meat.'

'But the native cats have taken the fowls,
They have na' left a leg;
And he'll get no omelette at all
Till the emu lays an egg!'

'Run down, run down, my little son, Jack,
To where the emus bide,
Ye shall find the old hen on the nest,
While the old cock sits beside.

'But speak them fair, and speak them soft,
Lest they kick ye a fearsome jolt.
Ye can gi' them a feed of thae half-inch nails
Or a rusty carriage bolt.'

So little son Jack ran blithely down
With the rusty nails in hand,
Till he came where the emus fluffed and scratched,
By their nest in the open sand.

And there he has gathered the new-laid egg,
Would feed three men or four,
And the emus came for the half-inch nails
Right up to the settler's door.

'A waste o' food,' said the dour gude wife,
As she took the egg, wi' a frown,
'But he gets no meat, unless ye run
A paddy-melon down.'

'Gae oot, gae oot, my little son Jack,
Wi' your twa-three doggies small;
Gin ye come not back wi' a paddy-melon,
Then come not back at all.'

So little son Jack he raced and he ran,
And he was bare o' the feet,
And soon he captured the paddy-melon,
Was gorged wi' the stolen wheat.

'Sit down, sit down, my bonny wee man,
To the best that the house can do—
An omelette made of the Emu egg
And a Paddy-melon stew.'

"Tis well, 'tis well,' said the bonny wee man;
'I have eaten the wide world's meat,
But the food that is given wi' right good will
Is the sweetest food to eat.

'But the night draws on to the Christmas Day
And I must rise and go,
For I have a mighty way to ride
To the land of the Esquimaux.

'And it's there I must load my sledges up,
With the reindeers four-in-hand,
That go to the north, south, east, and west,
To every Christian land.'

'Tae the Esquimaux,' said the dour good wife,
'Ye suit my husband well!
For when he gets up on his journey horse
He's a bit of a liar himsel'.'

Then out with a laugh went the bonny wee man
To his old horse grazing nigh,
And away like a meteor flash they went
Far off to the northern sky.

❖ ❖ ❖

When the children woke on the Christmas morn
They chattered with might and main—
Wi' a sword and gun for little son Jack,
And a braw new doll had Jane,
And a packet o' nails had the twa Emus;
But the dour gude wife gat nane.

Australian Town and Country Journal, 1906

The Shearer's Wife

Louis Esson

The dark—but drudgin's never done;
Now after tea inside the door
I patch an' darn from set o' sun,
Till hands git stiff and eyes grow sore,
   While Dick's outback.
And times I lie awake o' nights
An' watch the moon throw tricksy lights
An' shadows skeer with creepy sights
   Out in the ranges black.

Before the glare o' dawn I rise
To milk the sleepy cows, an' feed
The chooky-hens I dearly prize:
I set the bunny traps, then knead
    The weekly bread.
There's hay to stook, an' spuds to hoe,
An' ferns to cut in the scrub below,
An' I lay out palin's row on row
    To make a new cow-shed.

The poorness of this Savage Bush
Has crushed us since we came from town,
(To-night I'm dreamin' through the hush:
My eyes are bright, my hair's still brown,
    And I'm Young Lil.
'We'll have a farm,' Dick used to say,
'Where we'll be happy all the day,'
But now I'm wrinkled, worn, an' grey,
    And Dick's a shearer still.)

Blurred runs the track whereon he comes,
And tired am I with labour sore;
Tired o' the bush, an' cows, an' gums,
Tired—an' I want to think no more.
    What tales he tells
The moon is lonesome in the sky,
The bush is lone, and lonesome I
But Stare as the red dust clouds whirl by,
    And start at the cattle bells.

The Bulletin, 1907

A Snake Yarn

WT Goodge

'You talk of snakes,' said Jack the Rat,
'But blow me, one hot summer,
I seen a thing that knocked me flat—
Fourteen foot long or more than that.
It was a reg'lar hummer!
Lay right along a sort of bog,
   Just like a log!

'The ugly thing was lyin' there
And not a sign o' movin',
Give any man a nasty scare;
Seen nothin' like it anywhere
Since I first started drovin'.
And yet it didn't scare my dog.
   Looked like a log!

'I had to cross that bog, yer see,
And bluey I was humpin';
But wonderin' what that thing could be
A-lyin' there in front o' me
I didn't feel like jumpin'.
Yet, though I shivered like a frog,
   It *seemed* a log!

'I takes a leap and lands right on
The back of that there whopper!'
He stopped. We waited. Then Big Mac
Remarked: 'Well, then, what happened, Jack?'
'Not much,' said Jack, and drained his grog.
   'It *was* a log!'

The Bulletin, 1899

Song of the Artesian Waters

Banjo Paterson

Now the stock have started dying, for the Lord has sent a drought;
But we're sick of prayers and Providence—we're going to do without;
With the derricks up above us and the solid earth below,
We are waiting at the lever for the word to let her go.
   Sinking down, deeper down;
   Oh, we'll sink it deeper down.
As the drill is plugging downward at a thousand feet of level,
If the Lord won't send us water, oh, we'll get it from the devil;
Yes, we'll get it from the devil deeper down.

Now, our engine's built in Glasgow by a very canny Scot,
And he marked it twenty horse-power, but he don't know what is what.
When Canadian Bill is firing with the sun-dried gidgee logs,
She can equal thirty horses and a score or so of dogs.
   Sinking down, deeper down,
   Oh, we're going deeper down.
If we fail to get the water then it's ruin to the squatter,
For the drought is on the station and the weather's growing hotter;
But we're bound to get the water deeper down.

But the shaft has started caving and the sinking's very slow,
And the yellow rods are bending in the water down below,

And the tubes are always jamming and they can't be made to shift
Till we nearly burst the engine with a forty horse-power lift.
   Sinking down, deeper down,
   Oh, we're going deeper down.
Though the shaft is always caving, and the tubes are always jamming,
Yet we'll fight our way to water while the stubborn drill is ramming—
While the stubborn drill is ramming deeper down.

But there's no artesian water, though we've passed three thousand feet,
And the contract price is growing and the boss is nearly beat.
But it must be down beneath us, and it's down we've got to go,
Though she's bumping on the solid rock four thousand feet below.
   Sinking down, deeper down;
   Oh, we're going deeper down,
And it's time they heard us knocking on the roof of Satan's dwellin';
But we'll get artesian water if we cave the roof of hell in—
Oh! we'll get artesian water deeper down.

But it's hark! the whistle's blowing with a wild, exultant blast,
And the boys are madly cheering, for they've struck the flow at last,
And it's rushing up the tubing from four thousand feet below,
Till it spouts above the casing in a million-gallon flow.
   And it's down, deeper down—
   Oh, it comes from deeper down;

It is flowing, ever flowing, in a free, unstinted measure
From the silent hidden places where the old earth hides
    her treasure—
Where the old earth hides her treasure deeper down.

And it's clear away the timber, and it's let the water run:
How it glimmers in the shadow, how it flashes in the sun!
By the silent belts of timber, by the miles of blazing plain
It is bringing hope and comfort to the thirsty land again.
    Flowing down, further down;
    It is flowing further down
To the tortured thirsty cattle, bringing gladness in its
    going;
Through the droughty days of summer it is flowing, ever
    flowing—
It is flowing, ever flowing,
    further down.

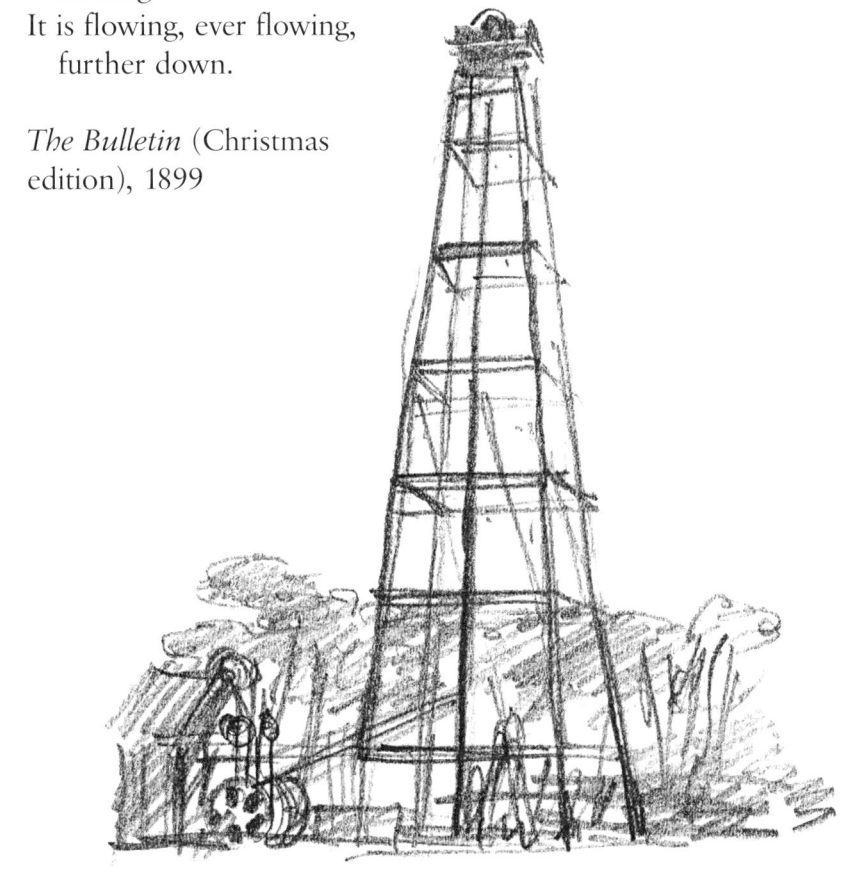

The Bulletin (Christmas edition), 1899

The Swagman

CJ Dennis

Oh, he was old and he was spare;
His bushy whiskers and his hair
Were all fussed up and very grey.
He said he'd come a long, long way
And had a long, long way to go.
Each boot was broken at the toe,
And he'd a swag upon his back.
His billy-can, as black as black,
Was just the thing for making tea
At picnics, so it seemed to me.

'Twas hard to earn a bite of bread,
He told me. Then he shook his head,
And all the little corks that hung
Around his hat-brim danced and swung
And bobbed about his face; and when
I laughed he made them dance again.
He said they were for keeping flies—
'The pesky varmints'—from his eyes.
He called me 'Codger' ... 'Now you see
The best days of your life,' said he.
'But days will come to bend your back,
And, when they come, keep off the track.
Keep off, young codger, if you can.'
He seemed a funny sort of man.

He told me that he wanted work,
But jobs were scarce this side of Bourke,
And he supposed he'd have to go
Another fifty mile or so.
'Nigh all my life the track I've walked,'
He said. I liked the way he talked.

> *A Book for Kids* was first published in 1921 and then republished as *Roundabout* in 1935. This poem was possibly CJ Dennis's favourite.

THE SWAGMAN

And oh, the places he had seen!
I don't know where he had not been—
On every road, in every town,
All through the country, up and down.
'Young codger, shun the track,' he said.
And put his hand upon my head.
I noticed, then, that his old eyes
Were very blue and very wise.
'Ay, once I was a little lad,'
He said, and seemed to grow quite sad.

I sometimes think: When I'm a man,
I'll get a good black billy-can
                      And hang some corks around my hat,
                          And lead a jolly life like that.

A Book for Kids, 1921

Tangmalangaloo

PJ Hartigan (John O'Brien)

The bishop sat in lordly state and purple cap sublime,
And galvanized the old bush church at Confirmation time.
And all the kids were mustered up from fifty miles around,
With Sunday clothes, and staring eyes, and ignorance profound.
Now was it fate, or was it grace, whereby they yarded too
An overgrown two-storey lad from Tangmalangaloo?

A hefty son of virgin soil, where nature has her fling,
And grows the trefoil three feet high and mats it in the spring;
Where mighty hills uplift their heads to pierce the welkin's rim,
And trees sprout up a hundred feet before they shoot a limb;
There everything is big and grand, and men are giants too—
But Christian Knowledge wilts, alas, at Tangmalangaloo.

The bishop summed the youngsters up, as bishops only can;
He cast a searching glance around, then fixed upon his man.
But glum and dumb and undismayed through every bout he sat;
He seemed to think that he was there, but wasn't sure of that.
The bishop gave a scornful look, as bishops sometimes do,
And glared right through the pagan in from Tangmalangaloo.

'Come, tell me, boy,' his lordship said in crushing tones
    severe,
'Come, tell me why is Christmas Day the greatest of
    the year?
'How is it that around the world we celebrate that day
'And send a name upon a card to those who're far away?
'Why is it wandering ones return with smiles and
    greetings, too?'
A squall of knowledge hit the lad from Tangmalangaloo.

He gave a lurch which set a-shake the vases on the shelf,
He knocked the benches all askew, up-ending of himself.
And so, how pleased his lordship was, and how he smiled
    to say,
'That's good, my boy. Come, tell me now; and what is
    Christmas Day?'
The ready answer bared a fact no bishop ever knew—
'It's the day before the races out at Tangmalangaloo.'

Around the Boree Log and other verses, 1922

The Teacher

CJ Dennis

I'd like to be a teacher, and have a clever brain,
Calling out, 'Attention, please!' and 'Must I speak in vain?'
I'd be quite strict with boys and girls whose minds I had
   to train,
And all the books and maps and things I'd carefully
   explain;
I'd make them learn the dates of kings, and all the capes
   of Spain;
   But I wouldn't be a teacher if . . .
      I couldn't use the cane.
         Would you?

A Book for Kids, 1921

THE TEACHER

The Teams

Henry Lawson

A cloud of dust on the long white road,
   And the teams go creeping on,
Inch by inch with the weary load;
And by the power of the green-hide goad
   The distant goal is won.

With eyes half-shut to the blinding dust,
   And necks to the yokes bent low,
The beasts are pulling as bullocks must,
And the shining rims of the tire-rings rust
   While the spokes are turning slow.

With face half-hid 'neath a broad-brimm'd hat
   That shades from the heat's white waves,
And shoulder'd whip with its green-hide plat,
The driver plods with a gait like that
   Of his weary, patient slaves.

He wipes his brow, for the day is hot,
   And spits to the left with spite;
He shouts at 'Bally', and flicks at 'Scot',
And raises dust from the back of 'Spot',
   And spits to the dusty right.

He'll sometimes pause as a thing of form
    In front of a lonely door,
And ask for a drink, and remark ''Tis warm,'
Or say 'There's signs of a thunder-storm;'
    But he seldom utters more.

But, ah! there are other scenes than these;
    And, passing his lonely home,
For weeks together the settler sees
The teams bogg'd down o'er the axletrees,
    Or ploughing the sodden loam.

And then when the roads are at their worst,
    The bushman's children hear
The cruel blows of the whips revers'd
While bullocks pull as their hearts would burst,
    And bellow with pain and fear.

And thus with little of joy or rest
    Are the long, long journeys done;
And thus—'tis a cruel war at the best—
Is distance fought in the lonely west,
    And the dusty battles won.

Australian Town and Country Journal, 1889

The Tram-Man

CJ Dennis

I'd like to be a Tram-man, and ride about all day,
Calling out, 'Fares, please!' in quite a 'ficious way,
With pockets full of pennies which I'd make
   the people pay.
But in the hottest days I'd take my tram down to the Bay;
And when I saw the nice cool sea I'd shout
   'Hip, hip, hooray!'
   But I wouldn't be a Tram-man if . . .
     I couldn't stop and play.
        Would you?

A Book for Kids, 1921

THE TRAM-MAN

The Traveller

CJ Dennis

As I rode in to Burrumbeet,
I met a man with funny feet;
And, when I paused to ask him why
His feet were strange, he rolled his eye
And said the rain would spoil the wheat;
So I rode on to Burrumbeet.

As I rode in to Beetaloo,
I met a man whose nose was blue;
And when I asked him how he got
A nose like that, he answered, 'What
Do bullocks mean when they say "Moo"?'
So I rode on to Beetaloo.

As I rode in to Ballarat,
I met a man who wore no hat;
And, when I said he might take cold,
He cried, 'The hills are quite as old
As yonder plains, but not so flat.'
So I rode on to Ballarat.

As I rode in to Gundagai,
I met a man and passed him by
Without a nod, without a word.
He turned, and said he'd never heard
Or seen a man so wise as I.
But I rode on to Gundagai.

THE TRAVELLER

As I rode homeward, full of doubt,
I met a stranger riding out:
A foolish man he seemed to me;
But, 'Nay, I am yourself,' said he,
'Just as you were when you rode out.'
So I rode homeward, free of doubt.

A Book for Kids, 1921

The Travelling Post-Office

Banjo Paterson

The roving breezes come and go, the reed-beds sweep and sway,
The sleepy river murmurs low, and loiters on its way;
It is the land of Lots o' Time—along the Castlereagh.

❖ ❖ ❖

The old man's son had left the farm—he found it dull and slow,
He drifted to the great North-west where all the rovers go.
'He's gone so long,' the old man said; 'he's dropped right out of mind,
But if you'd write a line to him I'd take it very kind.
He's shearing here and fencing there—a kind of waif and stray,
He's droving now with Conroy's sheep along the Castlereagh.

'The sheep are travelling for the grass and travelling very slow,
They may be at Mundooran now, or past the Overflow—
Or tramping down the black soil flats across by Waddiwong,
But all those little country towns would send the letter wrong.
The mailman, if he's extra-full, would pass them in his sleep—
It's safest to address the note to "care of Conroy's sheep,"
For five-and-twenty thousand head can scarcely go astray—
You write to "care of Conroy's sheep along the Castlereagh".'

❖ ❖ ❖

By rock and ridge and riverside the Western mail has gone,
Across the great Blue Mountain Range to take that letter on.
A moment on the topmost grade, while open fire-doors glare,
She pauses like a living thing to breathe the mountain air;
Then launches down the other side across the plains away
To bear that note to Conroy's sheep along the Castlereagh.

And now by coach and mailman's bag it goes from town
   to town,
And Conroy's Gap and Conroy's Creek have marked it 'further
   down.'
Beneath a sky of deepest blue, where never cloud abides,
A speck upon the waste of plain the lonely mailman rides;
Where fierce hot winds have set the pine and myall boughs
   asweep
He hails the shearers passing by for news of Conroy's sheep.
By big lagoons where wild-fowl play and crested pigeons flock,
By camp-fires where the drovers ride around their restless
   stock,
And past the teamster toiling down to fetch the wool away
My letter chases Conroy's sheep along the Castlereagh.

The Bulletin, 1894

The Triantiwontigongolope

CJ Dennis

There's a very funny insect that you do not often spy,
And it isn't quite a spider, and it isn't quite a fly;
It is something like a beetle, and a little like a bee,
But nothing like a woolly grub that climbs upon a tree.
Its name is quite a hard one, but you'll learn it soon, I hope.
So try:
  Tri-
    Tri-anti-wonti-
      Triantiwontigongolope.

It lives on weeds and wattle-gum, and has a funny face;
Its appetite is hearty, and its manners a disgrace.
When first you come upon it, it will give you quite a scare,
But when you look for it again, you find it isn't there.
And unless you call it softly it will stay away and mope.
So try:
  Tri-
    Tri-anti-wonti-
      Triantiwontigongolope.

It trembles if you tickle it or tread upon its toes;
It is not an early riser, but it has a snubbish nose.
If you sneer at it, or scold it, it will scuttle off in shame,
But it purrs and purrs quite proudly if you call it by its name,
And offer it some sandwiches of sealing-wax and soap.
So try:
  Tri-
    Tri-anti-wonti-
      Triantiwontigongolope.

But of course you haven't seen it; and I truthfully confess
That I haven't seen it either, and I don't know its address.
For there isn't such an insect, though there really might have been
If the trees and grass were purple, and the sky was bottle-green.
It's just a little joke of mine, which you'll forgive, I hope.
Oh, try!
  Tri!
    Tri-anti-wonti-
        Triantiwontigongolope.

A Book for Kids, 1921

Waiting for the Rain
(A Shearing Song)

John Neilson

The weather has been warm for a fortnight now or more,
And the shearers have been driving might and main,
For some have got the century who ne'er got it before;
But now all hands are waiting for the rain.

CHORUS
For the boss is getting rusty, and the ringer's caving in,
His bandaged wrist is aching with the pain,
And the second man, I fear, will make it hot for him
Unless we have another fall of rain.

Some are taking quarters and keeping well in bunk
While we shear the six-tooth wethers from the plain,
And if the sheep get harder some more of us will funk,
Unless we have another fall of rain.

Some cockies come here shearing; they would fill a little book
About this sad dry weather for the grain,
But here's lunch a-coming, make way for Dick the cook—
Old Dick is nigh as welcome as the rain.

But now the sky is overcast; the thunder's muttering loud;
The clouds are drifting westward o'er the plain,
And I see the red fire breaking from the edge of yonder cloud!
I hear the gentle patter of the rain!

So, lads, put on your stoppers, and let us to the hut,
We all can do a full day's rest again;

Some will be playing music, while some play ante-up,
And some are gazing outward at the rain.

❖ ❖ ❖

And now the rain is over let the pressers spin the screw,
Let the teamsters back their wagons in again,
We'll block the classers up by the way we put them
    through
For everything goes merry since the rain.

Let the boss bring out the bottle, let him 'wet' the final
    flock,
For the shearers here may ne'er meet all again;
Some may meet next season, but perhaps not even then
For soon we all will vanish
    like the rain.

The Men of the Fifties,
1938

Waltzing Matilda

Banjo Paterson

There once was a swagman camped in a billabong
Under the shade of a Coolibah tree
And he sang as he looked at the old billy boiling
Who'll come a-waltzing Matilda with me

Who'll come a-waltzing Matilda my darling
Who'll come a-waltzing Matilda with me
Waltzing Matilda and leading a water-bag
Who'll come a-waltzing Matilda with me

Down came a jumbuck to drink at
   the water-hole
Up jumped the swagman and grabbed
   him with glee
And he sang as he put him away in his
   tucker-bag
You'll come a-waltzing Matilda with me

You'll come a-waltzing Matilda
   my darling
You'll come a-waltzing Matilda with me
Waltzing Matilda and leading a water-bag
You'll come a-waltzing Matilda with me

Down came the squatter a-riding his
   thorough-bred
Down came policemen one two three
Whose is the jumbuck you've got in the
   tucker-bag
You'll come a-waltzing Matilda with me

You'll come a-waltzing Matilda my
   darling
You'll come a-waltzing Matilda with me
Waltzing Matilda and leading a water-bag
You'll come a-waltzing Matilda with me

But the swagman he up and he jumped
   in the water-hole
Drowning himself by the Coolibah tree
And his ghost may be heard as it sings by
   the billabong
      Who'll come a-waltzing Matilda
      with me.

> The Waltzing Matilda logo on the Australian $10 note is from a 1903 musical arrangement and was used to promote Billy Tea. Paterson wrote the first verse while holidaying in 1895 specifically to accompany a tune played by his friend Christina Macpherson. Her tune was probably based on a Scottish song. The version of 'Waltzing Matilda' most popular today first appeared in 1903. It is based on this version. A third version—the Queensland version—uses similar words but a different tune.

Waratah and Wattle

Henry Lawson

Though poor and in trouble I wander alone,
With a rebel cockade in my hat;
Though friends may desert me, and kindred disown,
My country will never do that!
You may sing of the Shamrock, the Thistle, and Rose,
Or the three in a bunch if you will;
But I know of a country that gathered all those,
And I love the great land where the Waratah grows,
And the Wattle-bough blooms on the hill.

Australia! Australia! so fair to behold—
While the blue sky is arching above;
The stranger should never have need to be told,
That the Wattle-bloom means that her heart is of gold,
And the Waratah red blood of love.

Australia! Australia! most beautiful name,
Most kindly and bountiful land;
I would die every death that might save her from shame,
If a black cloud should rise on the strand;
But whatever the quarrel, whoever her foes,
Let them come! Let them come when they will!
Though the struggle be grim, 'tis Australia that knows,
That her children shall fight while the Waratah grows,
And the Wattle blooms out on the hill.

When I was King, and other verses, 1905

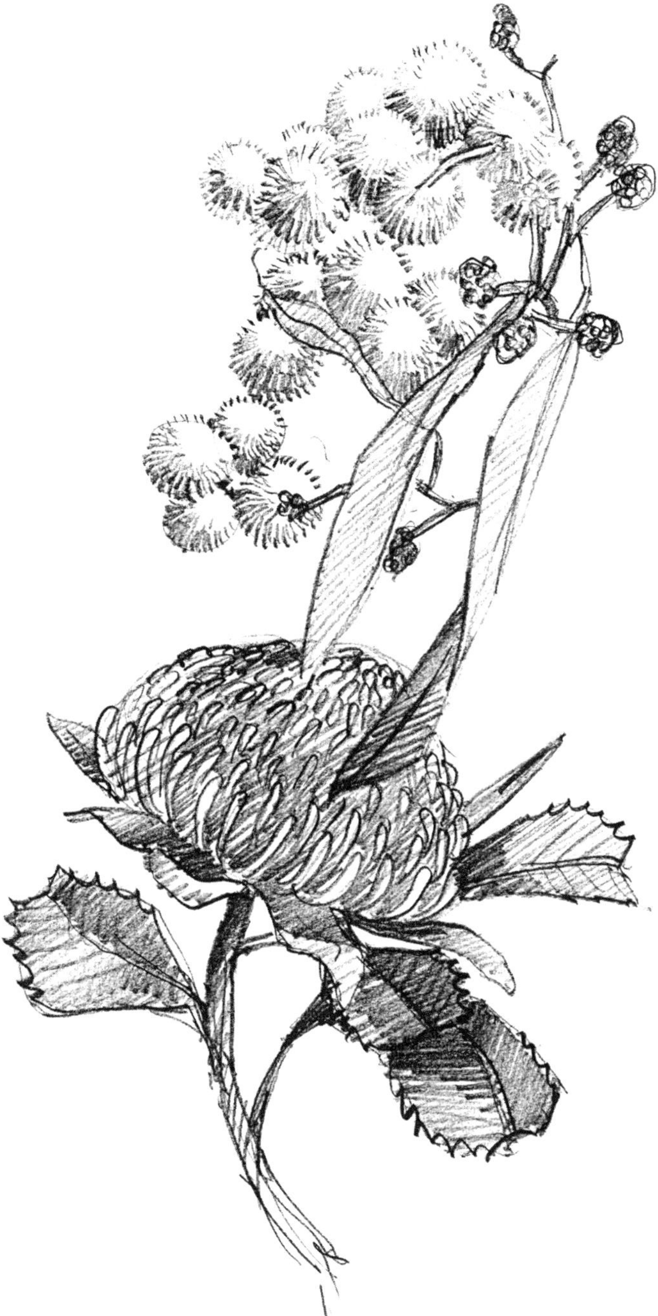

The Warrigal*

Henry Kendall

Through forest boles the stormwind rolls,
Vext of the sea-driv'n rain;
And, up in the clift, through many a rift,
The voices of torrents complain.
The sad marsh-fowl and the lonely owl
Are heard in the fog-wreaths grey,
When the warrigal wakes, and listens, and takes
To the woods that shelter the prey.

In the gully-deeps the blind creek sleeps,
And the silver, showery, moon
Glides over the hills, and floats, and fills,
And dreams in the dark lagoon;
While halting hard by the station yard,
Aghast at the hut-flame nigh,
The Warrigal yells—and the flats and fells
Are loud with his dismal cry.

On the topmost peak of mountains bleak
The south wind sobs, and strays
Through moaning pine, and turpentine,
And the rippling runnel ways;
And strong streams flow, and great mists go,

THE WARRIGAL

Where the Warrigal starts to hear
The watch-dog's bark break sharp in
  the dark,
And flees like a phantom of Fear!

The swift rains beat, and the thunders
  fleet
On the wings of the fiery gale,
And down in the glen of pool and fen,
The wild gums whistle and wail,
As over the plains and past the chains
Of waterholes glimmering deep,
The Warrigal flies from the Shepherd's cries,
And the clamour of dogs and sheep.

The Warrigal's lair is pent in bare
Black rocks at the gorge's mouth:
It is set in ways where Summer strays
With the sprites of flame and drouth;
But when the heights are touched with lights
Of hoarfrost, sleet, and shine,
His bed is made of the dead grass-blade
And the leaves of the windy pine.

He roves through the lands of sultry sands,
He hunts in the iron range,
Untamed as surge of the far sea verge,
And fierce and fickle and strange.
The white man's track and the haunts of the black
He shuns, and shudders to see;
For his joy he tastes in lonely wastes
Where his mates are torrent and tree.

Leaves from Australian Forests, 1869

* The Wild Dog

> This poem is often found starting with the lines *The Warrigal's lair* but in another edition Kendall begins with the current second verse!

Where the Dead Men Lie

Barcroft Henry Boake

Out on the wastes of the 'Never, Never,'
   That's where the dead men lie!
There where the heat-waves dance for ever,
   That's where the dead men lie;
That's where the earth's lov'd sons are keeping
Endless tryst—not the west wind sweeping
Feverish pinions can wake their sleeping—
   Out where the dead men lie.

Where brown Summer and Death have mated—
   That's where the dead men lie,
Loving with fiery lust unsated,
   That's where the dead men lie;
Out where the grinning skulls bleach whitely,
Under the saltbush sparkling brightly,
Out where the wild dogs chorus nightly,
   That's where the dead men lie.

Deep in the yellow, flowing river,
   That's where the dead men lie,
Under its banks where the shadows quiver,
   That's where the dead men lie;
Where the platypus twists and doubles,
Leaving a train of tiny bubbles;
Rid at last of their earthly troubles,
   That's where the dead men lie!

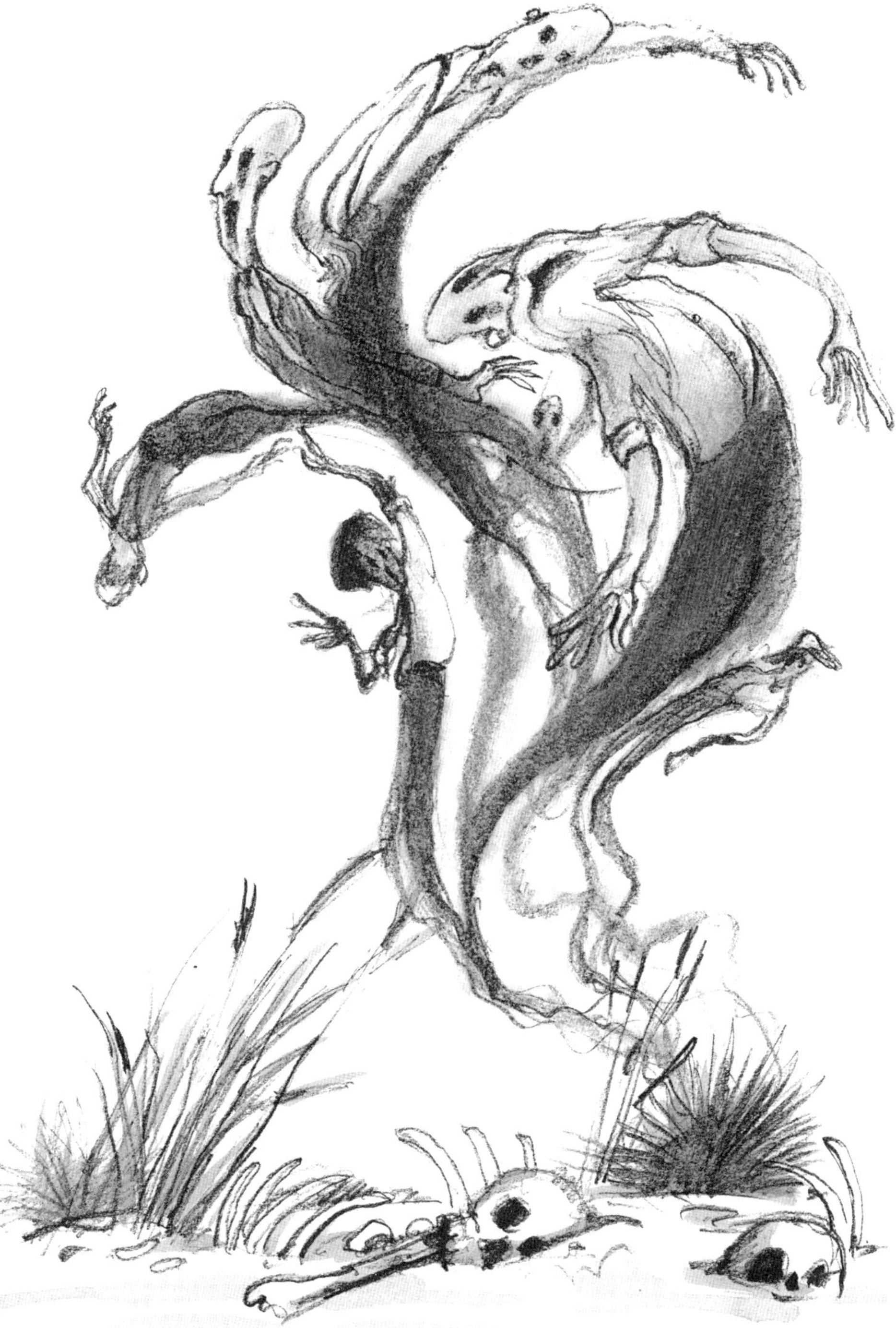

East and backward pale faces turning,
   That's how the dead men lie,
Gaunt arms stretched with a voiceless yearning,
   That's how the dead men lie.
Oft in the fragrant hush of nooning
Hearing again their mother's crooning,
Wrapt for aye in a dreamful swooning,
   That's how the dead men lie.

Naught but the hand of night can free them;
   That's when the dead men fly;
Only the frightened cattle see them—
   See the dead men go by;
Cloven hoofs beating out one measure,
Bidding the stockmen know no leisure,
That's where the dead men take their pleasure,
   That's when the dead men fly.

Ask too, the never-sleeping drover,
   He sees the dead pass by,
Hearing them call to their friends—the plover,
   Hearing the dead men cry.
Seeing their faces stealing, stealing,
Hearing their laughter, pealing, pealing,
Watching their grey forms wheeling, wheeling
   Round where the cattle lie.

Strangled by thirst and fierce privation,
   That's how the dead men die!
Out on 'Moneygrub's' farthest station,
   That's how the dead men die!
Hardfaced greybeards, youngsters callow,
Some mounds cared for, others fallow,
Some deep down, yet others shallow,
   Some having but the sky.

'Moneygrub,' as he sips his claret,
   Looks with complacent eye
Down at his watch-chain, eighteen-carat,
   There, in his club, hard by;
Recks not that every link is stamped with
Names of the men whose limbs are cramped with
Too long lying in grave mould, camped with
   Death where the dead men lie.

The Bulletin (Christmas edition), 1891

> The title for this poem in the original manuscript is 'Where the Dead Lie'. It was first printed in *The Bulletin* on 19 December, 1891 as 'Where the Dead Men Lie'. Boake himself was dead five months later.

Where the Pelican Builds

Mary Hannay Foott

[The unexplored parts of Australia are sometimes spoken of by the bushmen of Western Queensland as the home of the pelican, a bird whose nesting-place, so far as the writer knows, is seldom, if ever found.]

The horses were ready, the rails were down,
But the riders lingered still,—
One had a parting word to say,
And one had his pipe to fill.
Then they mounted, one with a granted prayer,
And one with a grief unguessed.
'We are going,' they said, as they rode away—
'Where the pelican builds her nest!'

They had told us of pastures wide and green,
To be sought past the sunset's glow;
Of rifts in the ranges by opal lit;
And gold 'neath the river's flow.
And thirst and hunger were banished words
When they spoke of that unknown West;
No drought they dreaded, no flood they feared,
Where the pelican builds her nest!

The creek at the ford was but fetlock deep
When we watched them crossing there;
The rains have replenished it twice since then,
And thrice has the rock lain bare.
But the waters of Hope have flowed and fled,
And never from blue hill's breast
Come back—by the sun and the sands devoured—
Where the pelican builds her nest!

The Bulletin, 1881

WHERE THE PELICAN BUILDS

'Where the Pelican Builds' is Hannay Foott's most famous poem and comes from the collection *Where the Pelican Builds*, published in 1885. This poem is about the legendary paradise in the centre of Australia where they thought there was an inland sea... where the pelican builds her nest.

The Women of the West

George Essex Evans

They left the vine-wreathed cottage and the mansion on the hill,
The houses in the busy streets where life is never still,
The pleasures of the city, and the friends they cherished best:
For love they faced the wilderness—the Women of the West.

The roar, and rush, and fever of the city died away,
And the old-time joys and faces—they were gone for many a day;
In their place the lurching coach-wheel, or the creaking bullock chains,
O'er the everlasting sameness of the never-ending plains.

In the slab-built, zinc-roofed homestead of some lately-taken run,
In the tent beside the bankment of a railway just begun,
In the huts on new selections—in the camps of man's unrest,
On the frontiers of the Nation, live the Women of the West.

The red sun robs their beauty and, in weariness and pain,
The slow years steal the nameless grace that never comes again;
And there are hours men cannot soothe, and words men cannot say—
The nearest woman's face may be a hundred miles away.

The wide Bush holds the secrets of their longing and desires,
When the white stars in reverence light their holy altar-fires,
And silence, like the touch of God, sinks deep into the breast—
Perchance He hears and understands the Women of the West.

For them no trumpet sounds the call, no poet plies his arts—
They only hear the beating of their gallant, loving hearts.
But they have sung with silent lives the song all songs above—
The holiness of sacrifice, the dignity of love.

Well have we held our fathers' creed. No call has passed us by.
We faced and fought the wilderness, we sent our sons to die.
And we have hearts to do and dare, and yet, o'er all the rest,
The hearts that made the Nation were the Women of the West.

The Brisbane Courier, 1901

Woolloomooloo

CJ Dennis

Here's a ridiculous riddle for you:
How many o's are in Woolloomooloo?
    Two for the W, two for the m,
    Four for the l's, and that's plenty for them.

A Book for Kids, 1921

Poet Biographies

Barcroft Henry Boake

Born: 26 March 1866, Balmain (NSW)
Died: 2 May 1892, Middle Harbour (NSW)

In his short life, **Barcroft Henry Thomas Boake** (who also wrote under the name Surcingle) was a surveyor's field assistant, boundary rider, drover, stockman, draftsman and poet. Many of his poems were first printed in *The Bulletin* and his first collection of poetry was not published until after his death. The unusual name Barcroft had been handed down through the family for generations. Boake loved the poetry of Adam Lindsay Gordon. He is buried at North Sydney cemetery.

CJ Dennis

Born: 7 September 1876, Auburn (South Australia)
Died: 22 June 1938, Melbourne (Victoria)

Clarence Michael James Dennis had a variety of jobs—including at a stock and station agency, as a bar tender, clerk, secretary to a senator, and journalist or editor for a number of newspapers, one of which he started—but it is his humorous stories and verse in major city newspapers for which he is most fondly remembered. Much of his writing appeared in *The Bulletin* and *The Herald*. After his early years growing up in South Australia, Dennis lived and worked in cities, including Melbourne, Sydney and Broken Hill. National memorials for Australia's 'laureate of the larrikin' are located in South Australia and in

Victoria. He is buried at Box Hill Cemetery. He also wrote under pseudonyms including 'The Den' and 'CJD'.

Edward Dyson

Born: 4 March 1865, Morrison (Victoria)
Died: 22 August 1931, Elwood (Victoria)

George Edward Dyson was a freelance writer. He was another writer who loved names, his pseudonyms including 'Billy T', 'Billy Tea', 'Silas Snell' and 'E.D.' His literary work included plays, stories, humorous verse, and jokes. He wrote in notebooks and on anything else that might be able to store his ideas. He also worked as a miner and in factories, but it was his experience growing up surrounded by the miners and the people he encountered while moving around early in life that became the source for much of his writing. He wrote for *The Bulletin* and many other papers.

Louis Esson

Born: 10 August 1878, Edinburgh (Scotland)
Died: 27 November 1943, Sydney (NSW)

Three-year-old **Thomas Louis Buvelot Esson** arrived in Australia with his mother and siblings after his father's death. He grew up in Melbourne. As an adult he worked as a library assistant and journalist, and also wrote plays and poems. He was passionate about the theatre. His work was often about being Australian and 'Australianness' and was published in *The Bulletin* and other newspapers. He travelled back to the land of his birth but returned to Australia a few years later, immersed himself in theatre and began publishing plays.

George Essex Evans

Born: 18 June 1863, London (England)
Died: 10 November 1909, Toowoomba (Queensland)

In 1881 at the age of eighteen, **George Essex Evans** migrated with his brother and two sisters to Queensland. He attempted farming at which he was unsuccessful. More success came as a teacher and then a journalist, editing and writing articles and stories. He also owned a newspaper and later worked as a public servant where he wrote books for the government tourist bureau. He was also a successful playwright. Essex's poetry, immensely patriotic and lovingly portraying the remote parts of Queensland, was written while he was employed in other occupations. It was sometimes written under the pseudonym of 'Christophus'. His poem 'Ode for Commonwealth Day' was entered into the inaugural Federation Day competition sponsored by the NSW government, and won the fifty-guinea first prize. Alfred Deakin, Australia's second Prime Minister, described Evans as Australia's national poet. Evans was buried at the Drayton and Toowoomba Cemetery and the Broken Column memorial was erected to his memory.

Mary Hannay Foott

Born: 26 September 1846, Glasgow (Scotland)
Died: 12 October 1918, Bundaberg (Queensland)

Mary Hannay Foott was just seven years old when her family arrived in Melbourne from Glasgow in 1853. She was a landowner, a schoolteacher, a governess, a journalist, an editor and writer of poems, plays and articles, and a licensed teacher of drawing. She studied art in Melbourne and used the income she gained from her writing to support her. After she married she lived in outback NSW in Bourke and later on the Paroo River in Queensland. Following her husband's death she moved with her young sons to Toowoomba and later Brisbane where she began writing for local newspapers. She eventually became an editor. Her poetry, often reflecting the landscape and her experiences of the places she had lived, appeared in newspapers and periodicals.

WT Goodge

Born: 28 September 1862, Middlesex (England)
Died: 28 November 1909, North Sydney (NSW)

At the age of eighteen, **William Thomas Goodge** took a job as a ship's steward and travelled to Sydney, where he decided to jump ship in 1882. He spent the next twelve years in outback NSW, where he was employed on some Cobb & Co. properties, but left and later became a newspaper journalist on regional newspapers. He eventually became an editor, freelance writer and part-owner of some newspapers. Much of his work was published in *The Bulletin*, as well as other newspapers. Only one collection, *Hits! Skits! and Jingles!* was published in his lifetime.

Adam Lindsay Gordon

Born: 19 October 1833, Fayal, Azores (Portugal)
Died: 24 June 1870, Brighton Beach (Victoria)

Growing up in England, **Adam Lindsay Gordon** was a restless youth (which is one way of saying that he got into a fair bit of trouble with the law). He emigrated to Adelaide in 1854 and, ironically, joined the South Australian mounted police. When he resigned from the force he successfully took up horse-breaking and riding horses in steeple chases. Gordon also became a South Australian Member of Parliament, later resigning and becoming a sheep farmer in Western Australia. His poetry, some of which was very romantic, was published in magazines Australia-wide. One collection was published the day before he died.

Gordon is buried at Brighton Cemetery in Victoria. In 1932 his statue was unveiled at Parliament House in Victoria and in 1934 he became the first Australian to have a memorial bust placed in Poet's Corner of Westminster Abbey.

PJ Hartigan (John O'Brien)

Born: 13 October 1878, Yass (NSW)
Died: 27 December 1952, Lewisham (NSW)

Patrick Joseph Hartigan was ordained as a Catholic priest in 1903 and was one of the first curates to have a motor car. He was an inspector of Catholic schools, a religious historian, a short story writer and (most famously) a poet. His early poetry (published in newspapers, the Catholic press and also *The Bulletin*) was written under the pen-name 'Mary Ann' while he was at the seminary. After his appointment as parish priest of Narrandera, he began writing as 'John O'Brien'. He loved the verse of Lawson and Paterson because their poems were of 'real' Australia and his own poetry also reflected his experience of Australia. He wrote about the struggle of life on the land, the humorous side of life, the bravery and endurance and the love of being Australian. When he died, a requiem Mass was said for him at Saint Mary's Cathedral. He is buried beside his parents in the North Rocks Cemetery.

Frank Hudson

Born: Unknown
Died: Unknown

Not much is known about **Frank Hudson**. His poetry has been published in *The Bulletin* and he probably lived in Australia in the early 1900s for a few years. He also spent some time in New Zealand and many years travelling the world.

Thomas Henry Kendall

Born: 18 April 1839, Milton (near Ulladulla) (NSW)
Died: 1 August 1882, Surry Hills (NSW)

Henry Kendall's first job was as a cabin boy on a whaling ship, but that only lasted for two years—the work was too hard! He was also a shop assistant and a civil servant. After his writing began to be published in newspapers and periodicals in Sydney and Melbourne, he became a journalist and editor. A period of ill health saw him take work as a bookkeeper. He loved writing about the

Australian bush, the coast and arid inland—and about the harshness of life for the early explorers. Kendall liked names. He was married as Henry Clarence Kendall (his birth name was Thomas Henry Kendall) and he wrote under names including 'A. Mopoke', 'A Literary Hack', and 'The Meddler'. He is buried in Waverley Cemetery (NSW) where a monument was erected to his memory in 1886.

Henry Lawson

Born: 17 June 1867, Grenfell (NSW)
Died: 2 September 1922, Abbotsford (NSW)

Born on the Grenfell goldfields, **Henry Lawson** had many occupations throughout his life. He was a journalist, novelist, short story writer, poet, shearer, coach painter and clerk. After his marriage he lived with his family in New Zealand and England for a time, although most of his life was spent in Australia. Lawson attended school for only about three years and a childhood illness left him partially deaf by the age of fourteen, yet he has become one of Australia's greatest literary figures. Much of his writing—both verse and stories—is about the good and the bad of the land, ordinary people, mateship and life in the outback. In September 1892, *The Bulletin* gave Lawson a rail ticket and a small amount of money. The destination was Bourke in western NSW and it was this time experiencing outback life that provided the material for much of his most famous writing. He was the first writer to be given a state funeral.

John Neilson

Born: 15 January 1845 (probably; some say 1844), Stranraer (Scotland)
Died: 1922, Leongatha (Victoria)

John Neilson was the father of the poet John Shaw Neilson. Like his son he had little schooling and worked throughout his life in many labour-intensive jobs. He was also a successful bush poet. His verse appeared in local newspapers and magazines. In 1893 he and his son John Shaw Neilson entered the Australian Natives Association poetry competition. They both won first prize in their respective sections.

It wasn't until after his death that a collection of his verse was published, in 1938.

John Shaw Neilson

Born: 22 February 1872, Penola (South Australia)
Died: 12 May 1942, Footscray (Victoria)

John Shaw Neilson had very little schooling (totalling possibly two years); he read little and had poor eyesight. He often worked with his brothers and father in occupations that required lots of manual labour, such as road work, fencing, timber-cutting and scrub-clearing. He worked as a farmer and also a public servant. Working outdoors helped Neilson to observe, listen and interact with the environment around him. Some of his poetry showed his love for nature. His happiest years were when he left the bush and settled in Melbourne. Neilson had started writing poetry when he left school and his poetry appeared in papers; *The Bulletin* began to publish his verse in 1895. He had five books of poetry published during his life. Much of his verse was created in his head before being dictated, often to his family, because of his poor eyesight. Most of Neilson's writing (including letters, lists, outlines for poems and household notes) was recorded in twenty-eight notebooks. Some of his work has been set to music and recorded.

Neilson is buried in Footscray cemetery and a bust of him is on display at Footscray Library.

AB (Banjo) Paterson

Born: 17 February 1864, Narrambla (NSW)
Died: 5 February 1941, Sydney (NSW)

Andrew Barton Paterson had many occupations throughout his life including solicitor, army officer during World War I, *Sydney Morning Herald* war correspondent during the Boer War and in China, journalist and novelist, but he is mainly remembered as one of Australia's most famous bush poets. He had a lifelong love of horses and the outdoors and this showed in his wonderful ballads of Australian life, the landscape and his passion for Australia. His first poem appeared in 1885 in *The Bulletin*, where many of his works were published, often under the pseudonym of 'B' or 'the Banjo' which was probably the name of a family racehorse. In 1938 he was appointed CBE (Commander of the Order of the British Empire) for his services to Australian literature. He was known as 'Barty' to family and friends but to most Australians he is known as 'Banjo'.

GM Smith

Born: Unknown
Died: Unknown

Very little is known about **GM Smith**. He also wrote as 'Steele Grey'. He co-wrote a history book about World War I.

Thomas E Spencer

Born: 30 December 1845, London (England)
Died: 6 May 1911, Glebe Point (NSW)

Thomas Edward Spencer arrived in Sydney in 1875. He was a stonemason by trade, but was also employed as a building contractor, and as a representative for the Court of Arbitration. The verse and prose that he wrote, some for *The Bulletin*, was created for his own enjoyment. This too was very successful. Some of his work was written under the names 'McSweeney' and 'Mrs Bridget'. Spencer is buried at Rookwood Cemetery in Sydney.

DH Souter

Born: 30 March 1862, Aberdeen (Scotland)
Died: 22 September 1935, Bondi (NSW)

David Henry Souter was born in Scotland, moved to South Africa in 1881 and finally settled in Sydney in about 1887. He was one of the first book-plate designers but he was also a poster artist, composer, illustrator, editor, journalist and poet. He is best known for the cartoons and sketches that he created for *The Bulletin* magazine where he had one cartoon published in every edition for forty years from 1895. The 'Souter cat' is a feature of many of his sketches and possibly originated as an inkblot. Even a child's chair he owned was decorated with a carved and painted image of the black cat!

Book References

WT Goodge, *Hits! Skits! & Jingles!* The Bulletin Newspaper Company, Sydney, 1904

Mary Hannay Foott, *Where the Pelican Builds and other poems*, Gordon & Gotch, Brisbane, 1885

Henry Kendall, *The Poems of Henry Kendall* (with biographical note by Bertram Stevens), Angus & Robertson, Sydney, 1920

DH Souter, *Bush-Babs:* with pictures, Endeavour Press, Sydney, 1933

Also

Barcroft Henry Boake, *Where the Dead Men Lie and other poems*, Angus & Robertson, Sydney, 1897

CJ Dennis, *A Book for Kids*, Angus & Robertson, Sydney, 1921 & http://nla.gov.au/nla.aus-f2678

Louis Esson, *Bells and Bees*, Lothian, Melbourne, 1910

George Essex Evans, *The Secret Key and other verses*, Angus & Robertson, Sydney, 1906

Adam Lindsay Gordon, *Poems of Adam Lindsay Gordon*, Edited with introductory notes by Frank Maldon Robb, Oxford University Press, London, 1913

Henry Kendall, *Poems of Henry Kendall*, George Robertson & Co., Melbourne, 1886

John Neilson, *The Men of the Fifties*, Hawthorne Press, Melbourne, 1938

John Shaw Neilson, *Collected Poems of John Shaw Neilson*, Edited with an introduction by RH Croll, Lothian Book Publishing Co., Melbourne, 1934

John O'Brien (PJ Hartigan), *Around the Boree Log and other verses*, Angus & Robertson, Sydney, 1922

AB Paterson, *The Animals Noah Forgot*, Endeavour Press, Sydney, 1933

GM Smith (Steele Grey), *The Days of Cobb & Co. and other verses*, Federal Printing Works, Parramatta, 1906

Thomas E Spencer, *The Bulletin Reciter: a collection of verses for recitation from* The Bulletin, NSW Bookstall Co., Sydney, 1901

Index of First Lines

A cloud of dust on the long white road	110
A peaceful spot is Piper's Flat. The folk that live around—	44
A pleasant shady place it is, a pleasant place and cool—	68
A short time back while over in Vic	82
As I rode in to Burrumbeet	114
Australia's a big country	34
By channels of coolness the echoes are calling	16
Did you see them pass to-day, Billy, Kate and Robin	41
Each poet that I know (he said)	80
Far from the trouble and toil of town	72
Fire-lighted, on the table a meal for sleepy men	50
Have you seen the bush by moonlight, from the train, go running by?	73
He crouches, and buries his face on his knees	48
Here's a ridiculous riddle for you	136
Hey, there! Hoop-la! the circus is in town!	25
Hist! . . . . . . Hark! The night is very dark	42
I had written him a letter which I had, for want of better	26
I have a trim typewriter now	66
I'd like to be a pieman, and ring a little bell	75
I'd like to be a teacher, and have a clever brain	108
I'd like to be a Tram-man, and ride about all day	112
It chanced out back at the Christmas time	94
It lies beyond the Western Pines	18
It was somewhere up the country, in a land of rock and scrub	38
It was the man from Ironbark who struck the Sydney town	54
Mr Smith of Tallabung	62
Now the stock have started dying, for the Lord has sent a drought	101
Oh there once was a swagman camped in the billabong	122
Oh, he was old and he was spare	104
On the blue plains in wintry days	67

On the outer Barcoo where the churches are few	20
On the Sunday morning mustered	78
Once a little sugar ant made up his mind to roam—	10
Our Andy's gone to battle now	8
Out on the wastes of the 'Never Never'	128
Scrape the bottom of the hole, gather up the stuff	30
The baker-man was kneading dough	74
The bell is set a-ringing, and the engine gives a toot	14
The bishop sat in lordly state and purple cap sublime	106
The dark—but drudgin's never done	98
The Emus formed a football team	36
The horses were ready, the rails were down	132
The night too quickly passes	84
The ocean heaves around us still	32
The roving breezes come and go, the reed beds sweep and sway	116
The sun burns hotly thro' the gums	22
The weather has been warm for a fortnight now or more	120
There was movement at the station, for the word had passed around	56
There's a very funny insect that you do not often spy	118
They came of bold and roving stock that would not fixed abide	77
They left the vine-wreathed cottage and the mansion on the hill	134
Though poor and in trouble I wander alone	124
Through forest boles the stormwind rolls	126
'Tis Spring! Sing hey!	88
'Tis the everyday Australian	12
'Twas Mulga Bill, from Eaglehawk, that caught the cycling craze	64
We are the old-world people	76
We have Telephones and Cables	28
'We'll all be rooned,' said Hanrahan	90
'You talk of snakes,' said Jack the Rat	100

Index of Poets

Author	Poem Title
Barcroft Henry Boake	The Digger's Song
Barcroft Henry Boake	Where the Dead Men Lie
CJ Dennis	Hist!
CJ Dennis	The Ant Explorer
CJ Dennis	A Bush Christmas
CJ Dennis	The Circus
CJ Dennis	Going to School
CJ Dennis	The Pieman
CJ Dennis	Poets
CJ Dennis	A Ruined Reversolet
CJ Dennis	The Swagman
CJ Dennis	The Teacher
CJ Dennis	The Tram-Man
CJ Dennis	The Traveller
CJ Dennis	The Triantiwontigongolope
CJ Dennis	Woolloomooloo
Edward Dyson	My Typewriter
Louis Esson	The Shearer's Wife
George Essex Evans	The Women of the West
Mary Hannay Foott	Where the Pelican Builds
WT Goodge	The Australian Slanguage
WT Goodge	'Ough!'
WT Goodge	A Snake Yarn
Adam Lindsay Gordon	An Exile's Farewell
PJ Hartigan (John O'Brien)	Pitchin' at the Church
PJ Hartigan (John O'Brien)	Said Hanrahan
PJ Hartigan (John O'Brien)	Tangmalangaloo
Frank Hudson	Pioneers
Henry Kendall	Bell-birds
Henry Kendall	The Last of His Tribe
Henry Kendall	The Warrigal
Henry Lawson	Andy's Gone With Cattle
Henry Lawson	Freedom on the Wallaby

Henry Lawson	The Lights of Cobb & Co.
Henry Lawson	On the Night Train
Henry Lawson	The Roaring Days
Henry Lawson	The Teams
Henry Lawson	Waratah and Wattle
John Neilson	Waiting for the Rain (A Shearing Song)
John Shaw Neilson	Native Companions Dancing
John Shaw Neilson	Old Granny Sullivan
Banjo Paterson	A Ballad of Shearing (Shearing at Castlereagh)
Banjo Paterson	Brumby's Run
Banjo Paterson	A Bush Christening
Banjo Paterson	Clancy of the Overflow
Banjo Paterson	Fur and Feathers
Banjo Paterson	The Geebung Polo Club
Banjo Paterson	The Man from Ironbark
Banjo Paterson	The Man from Snowy River
Banjo Paterson	Mulga Bill's Bicycle
Banjo Paterson	Old Man Platypus
Banjo Paterson	Pioneers
Banjo Paterson	Santa Claus in the Bush
Banjo Paterson	Song of the Artesian Waters
Banjo Paterson	The Travelling Post-Office
Banjo Paterson	Waltzing Matilda
GM Smith (Steele Grey)	The Days of Cobb & Co.
GM Smith (Steele Grey)	Post-Hole Mick
Thomas E Spencer	How M'Dougal Topped the Score
DH Souter	Mr Smith

Poem   Reference

Poem	Reference
Andy's Gone With Cattle	*Australian Town and Country Journal*; vol. 38 no. 979, 13 October 1888 (p 757)
Ant Explorer, The	*A Book for Kids,* Angus and Robertson, Sydney, 1921
Australian Slanguage, The	*The Bulletin* vol. 19 no. 955, 4 June 1898, The Red Page (p 2)
Ballad of Shearing, A (Shearing at Castlereagh)	*The Bulletin* vol. 14 no. 730, 10 February 1894 (p 20)
Bell-birds	*Poems of Henry Kendall,* George Robertson & Co., Melbourne, 1886
Brumby's Run	*The Bulletin* vol. 16 no. 827, 21 December 1895 (p 27)
Bush Christening, A	*The Bulletin* (Christmas edition) vol. 13 no. 722, 16 December 1893 (p 16)
Bush Christmas, A	*The Herald,* 24 December 1931, (p 4)
Circus, The	*A Book for Kids*, Angus & Robertson, Sydney, 1921
Clancy Of The Overflow	*The Bulletin* (Christmas edition) vol. 10 no. 514; 21 December 1889
Days of Cobb & Co., The	*The Days of Cobb & Co. and other verses*; Federal Printing Works, Parramatta, 1906
Digger's Song, The	*The Bulletin* vol. 11 no. 611, 31 October 1891 (p 22)

Exile's Farewell, An	*Poems of Adam Lindsay Gordon*, Oxford University Press, London, 1913
Freedom on the Wallaby	*The Worker*, Federated Workers of Queensland, Brisbane, 16 May 1891 (p 8)
Fur and Feathers	*The Animals Noah Forgot*, Endeavour Press, Sydney, 1933
Geebung Polo Club, The	*The Antipodean*, George Robertson & Co., Melbourne, December 1893
Going to School	*A Book for Kids*, Angus & Robertson, Sydney, 1921
Hist!	*A Book for Kids*, Angus & Robertson, Sydney, 1921
How M'Dougal Topped the Score	*The Bulletin* vol. 19 no. 943, 12 March 1898
Last of His Tribe, The	*Poems of Henry Kendall*, George Robertson & Co., Melbourne, 1886
Lights of Cobb and Co., The	*The Bulletin* (Christmas edition) vol. 18 no. 930, 11 December 1897 (p 7)
Man From Ironbark, The	*The Bulletin* (Christmas edition) vol. 12 no. 670, 17 December 1892 (p 1)
Man From Snowy River, The	*The Bulletin* vol. 11 no.532; 26 April 1890 (p 13)
Mr Smith	*Bush-Babs*: with pictures, Endeavour Press, Sydney, 1933
Mulga Bill's Bicycle	*The Sydney Mail*, 25 July 1896
My Typewriter	*The Bulletin* vol. 38 no. 1960, 6 September 1917 (p 45)

Native Companions Dancing	*Collected Poems of John Shaw Neilson*, Lothian, Melbourne, 1934
Old Granny Sullivan	*The Bookfellow*, 17 January 1907 (p 8)
Old Man Platypus	*The Animals Noah Forgot*, Endeavour Press, Sydney, 1933
On the Night Train	*Birth, A Little Journal of Australian Poetry* vol. 6 no. 64, March 1922 (p 25)
'Ough!'	*The Bulletin*, vol 27 no. 1372, 31 May 1906
Pieman, The	*A Book for Kids*, Angus & Robertson, Sydney, 1921
Pioneers	*The Song of Manly Men and other verses*, David Nutt, 1908
Pioneers	*Australian Town and Country Journal* vol. 53 no. 1402, 19 December 1896
Pitchin' at the Church	*Around the Boree Log and other verses*, Angus & Robertson, Sydney, 1922
Poets	*The Herald*, 22 December 1936
Post-Hole Mick	*The Days of Cobb & Co. and other verses*; Federal Printing Works, Parramatta, 1906
Roaring Days, The	*The Bulletin* (Christmas edition) vol. 10 no. 514, 21 December 1889 (p 26)
Ruined Reversolet, A	*The Bulletin* vol. 29 no. 1505, 17 December, 1908, The Red Page (p 2)

Said Hanrahan	*Around the Boree Log and other verses*, Angus & Robertson, Sydney, 1922
Santa Claus in the Bush	*Australian Town and Country Journal* vol. 73 no. 1923, 12 December 1906 (p 34)
Shearer's Wife, The	*The Bulletin* vol. 28 no. 1431, 18 July 1907 (p 14)
Snake Yarn, A	*The Bulletin* vol. 19 no. 988, 21 January 1899 (p 14)
Song of the Artesian Waters	*The Bulletin* (Christmas edition) vol. 17 no. 878, 12 December 1896 (p 10)
Swagman, The	*A Book for Kids*, Angus & Robertson, Sydney, 1921
Tangmalangaloo	*Around the Boree Log and other verses*, Angus & Robertson, Sydney, 1922
Teacher, The	*A Book for Kids*, Angus & Robertson, Sydney, 1921
Teams, The	*Australian Town and Country Journal* vol. 39 no. 1040, 21 December 1889 (p 16)
Tram-Man, The	*A Book for Kids*, Angus & Robertson, Sydney, 1921
Traveller, The	*A Book for Kids*, Angus & Robertson, Sydney, 1921
Travelling Post-Office, The	*The Bulletin* vol. 14 no. 734, 10 March 1894 (p 20)
Triantiwontigongolope, The	*A Book for Kids*, Angus & Robertson, Sydney, 1921
Waiting for the Rain	*The Men of the Fifties*, Hawthorn Press, Melbourne, 1938

Waltzing Matilda	http://www.nla.gov.au/apps/cdview?pi=nla.ms-ms9065-2
Waratah and Wattle	*When I was King and other verses*, Angus & Robertson, Sydney, 1905
Warrigal, The	*Leaves from Australian Forests*, George Robertson, Melbourne, 1869
Where the Dead Men Lie	*The Bulletin* (Christmas edition) vol. 11 no. 618, 19 December 1891 (p 7)
Where the Pelican Builds	*The Bulletin* vol. 5 no. 59, 12 March 1881 (p 9)
Women of the West, The	*The Brisbane Courier* 14 September 1901 (p 13)
Woolloomooloo	*A Book for Kids*, Angus & Robertson, Sydney, 1921

About the Editor

Christopher Cheng worked as a teacher in city and country schools before moving to Taronga Zoo as an education officer for eight years, establishing Australia's first Zoomobile. He has been National Children's Development Manager at Dymocks and Education Advisor for the BioScope Initiative, a science-based CD-ROM project at Purdue University, USA.

Chris has a Master of Arts in Children's Literature and has been a Literacy Ambassador for the Federal Government's Literacy and Numeracy Week initiative.

He is an accomplished children's author who writes fiction and non-fiction full time, conducts workshops and visits schools. He has also presented to students at schools and universities in the USA. His picture book *One child*, illustrated by Steven Woolman, won the Wilderness Society Environment Award for Picture Books (Australia) and the 2000 Skipping Stones Honour Book (USA). He also wrote *30 Amazing Australian Animals* for Random House Australia and recently completed a libretto for a children's Christmas musical.

Chris lives in Sydney, Australia, near wonderful coffee shops and restaurants in a very old (newly renovated) terrace with his wife.

Find out more about Chris at www.chrischeng.com

About the Illustrator

Gregory Rogers studied fine art at the Queensland College of Art and has illustrated a large number of educational and trade children's picture books, including six books in the Random House *30 Australian . . .* series. In 1995 he won the Kate Greenaway Medal for his illustrations in *Way Home*. His first wordless picture book, *The Boy, the Bear, the Baron, the Bard*, was selected as one of the *New York Times*' Ten Best Illustrated Picture Books of 2004 and received numerous other awards and nominations. He also illustrated Nette Hilton's *Pyro Watson and the Hidden Treasure*, published by Woolshed Press, an imprint of Random House Australia.

Gregory lives in Brisbane, Australia.

To my primary school teachers, especially Kevin and Helen. CC
For Matt. GR

A Random House book
Published by Random House Australia Pty Ltd
Level 3, 100 Pacific Highway, North Sydney NSW 2060
www.randomhouse.com.au

First published by Random House Australia in 2009
This edition published in 2011

Copyright in this selection and arrangement © Christopher Cheng 2009
Copyright in the foreword and afterword © Christopher Cheng 2009
Illustrations copyright © Gregory Rogers 2009

The moral rights of the author and illustrator have been asserted.

All rights reserved. No part of this book may be reproduced or transmitted by any person or entity, including internet search engines or retailers, in any form or by any means, electronic or mechanical, including photocopying (except under the statutory exceptions provisions of the Australian *Copyright Act 1968*), recording, scanning or by any information storage and retrieval system without the prior written permission of Random House Australia.

Addresses for companies within the Random House Group can be found at www.randomhouse.com.au/offices.

Cataloguing-in-Publication entry is available from the National Library of Australia

ISBN 978 1 74275 362 1

Cover and internal illustrations by Gregory Rogers
Cover design by Christabella Designs
Internal design and typesetting by Anna Warren, Warren Ventures

Printed and bound in China by 1010 Printing International Limited